P9-CFB-263

14. Try, TRY!! not to check e-mail, texts, Facebook, Twitter, Google Alerts, or your horoscope while making a meal. Leaving the smartphone in another room helps.

15. Clean as you go. Even just washing the cutting board and wiping down the counter lessens the end-of-the-meal mess—and that sinking feeling when you see it.

16. Season like you mean it. We've had plenty of meals made with care that tasted like sawdust because the cook didn't add enough salt.

17. Taste your food before you serve it. Sounds obvious, except when all you want to do is get the food on the table. But what's the point if it has no flavor?

18. Julia Child said, "No matter what happens in the kitchen, never apologize." As usual, Julia's right.

19. Cooking for someone is an emotional act, so when other people cook for you—this does happen sometimes, right?—be sure to give them the same compliments that you'd like to hear.

20. Encourage your kids to help you cook, even if it's just grating cheese (they're much more inclined to eat food they've had a hand in making), but be realistic. If you're not in the mood, save it for a lazy Sunday.

21. Invite someone over for dinner on a weeknight. Sharing a casual, everyday meal with a friend or neighbor beats a fancy dinner party anytime.

22. Do your best to feed yourself and others with the most natural ingredients, the least fuss, and the most pleasure.

23. The best ingredient of all is a four-letter word. No, not wine. *Love*. Corny, but true.

KEEPERS

KEEPERS

Two Home Cooks Share
Their Tried-and-True Weeknight Recipes
and the Secrets to
Happiness in the Kitchen

KATHY BRENNAN AND
CAROLINE CAMPION

PHOTOGRAPHS BY CHRISTOPHER TESTANI

RODALE.

Mention of specific companies, organizations, or authorities in this book does not imply endorsement by the author or publisher, nor does mention of specific companies, organizations, or authorities imply that they endorse this book, its author, or the publisher.

Internet addresses and telephone numbers given in this book were accurate at the time it went to press.

© 2013 by Kathy Brennan and Caroline Campion

All rights reserved. No part of this publication may be reproduced or transmitted in any form or by any means, electronic or mechanical, including photocopying, recording, or any other information storage and retrieval system, without the written permission of the publisher.

Rodale books may be purchased for business or promotional use or for special sales. For information, please write to: Special Markets Department, Rodale Inc., 733 Third Avenue, New York, NY 10017.

Printed in the United States of America

Rodale Inc. makes every effort to use acid-free ∞, recycled paper ♻.

Book design by Kara Plikaitis

Photography by Christopher Testani

Illustrations by Kathy Brennan, Keiko Brennan, Sarah Brennan-Martin, Caroline Campion, and Ava Steinberger.

Library of Congress Cataloging-in-Publication Data is on file with the publisher.

ISBN-13: 978-1-60961-354-9

Distributed to the trade by Macmillan

2 4 6 8 10 9 7 5 3 1 hardcover

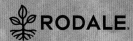

We inspire and enable people to improve their lives and the world around them.

rodalebooks.com

To my parents, who always put their kids (and grandkids) first and made sure our dinner table was filled with good food, spirited conversation, and bonhomie. —KB

To Tim, I cook with love because of you. —CC

CONTENTS

WHAT'S A KEEPER?

When we were editors at *Saveur* magazine, one of our favorite parts of the job was getting to taste the dishes that came out of the test kitchen. Some recipes worked better than others, but if the food editors came across one that was particularly wonderful, they'd announce, "It's a keeper!" By that, they didn't just mean the recipe was good enough to include in the magazine. To earn keeper status, a recipe also had to be foolproof, the best of its kind, and something you'd want to run home and make immediately.

We all need "keepers" in our life—brag-worthy, reliable, crowd-pleasing preparations that we confidently turn to again and again. That's especially true when it comes to weeknight meals. Even for people who adore cooking, who have no problem whipping up multi-course feasts on the weekend, the Monday-to-Friday dinner gauntlet can be challenging, even paralyzing. Despite all the food-related magazines, Web sites, blogs, books, and television shows, countless people still struggle whenever dinnertime arrives. We want family meals, to be able to put healthful food on the table, to use more fresh ingredients, to have a wide variety of dishes in their repertoire, and to enjoy the process more, but so many of us are being left behind in a vapor trail of truffle oil and dashi.

"What are you making for dinner tonight?" must be one of the most commonly asked questions Monday to Friday. Whether you're single and in charge of your own kitchen for the first time, one-half of a couple trying to get out of a jarred pasta sauce rut, a parent of young children looking for accessible recipes and a little handholding, or a parent of voracious teenagers who are costing you a small fortune in frozen burritos, chances are you've asked it. We have. Plenty of times. In fact, *Keepers* was born out of our own workplace conversations about dinner. At *Saveur*, we regularly talked about our mealtime woes. (Smuggling the test kitchen's leftovers home each day was unfortunately not a solution.)

Our afternoon desk-side conversations went something like this:

What are you making tonight?
I don't know, but I'm already starving. I feel like I need to make fish. We haven't had fish in ages.
Why don't you pick up some salmon on the way home and cook it in parchment?
You assume I have parchment paper.
Just use foil then.
Okay, and then what?
Toss together some baby spinach, minced shallots, and whatever fresh herbs you have, mound it on pieces of foil, then top it with a fillet, a little cream, salt, pepper, maybe some lemon zest. Roast at 425° for, like, 9 minutes.
Really—that's it? Sounds great, and I can serve it with leftover rice from the other night.
Done.

Those recipe swaps and pep talks were a lifeline. Anxiety loves company, and to know that someone else (particularly someone whose professional life revolved around food) was in the exact same situation was extremely reassuring. Many conversations later, we realized that by exchanging not only our best weeknight recipes but also our best cooking- and kitchen-related tips (make a big batch of beans on Sunday, *force* yourself to sketch out a menu for the week and shop for it in *one* go, chicken thighs reheat better than breasts, this is the only spatula you'll ever need!), we were helping each other, meal by meal, become better weeknight cooks. The thing we discovered was that quality weeknight meals don't require a big investment of time, money, or energy. With a little effort and planning (and realistic expectations), it was possible to do better.

Yes, we were fortunate to have picked up a lot of kitchen moves from our moms, grandmoms, culinary school for Kathy, and our jobs. But it really took (a lot of) individual trial and error, sharing our experiences, and encouraging each other to feel like we finally had mastered the Monday-to-Friday dinner challenge, and ultimately feel inspired to share what we'd learned with others.

At the heart of our book is a collection of recipes, more than 125 of our favorite original weeknight-friendly keepers—simple, trusted, satisfying dishes that are never boring. We've included streamlined classics, "international" and superfast dishes, ones that reheat well, and four categories of sides: starches and grains, hot vegetables, cold vegetables, and green salads. Rounding out the mix is a section devoted to sauces and dressings that we call Lifesavers because they're versatile, can be prepared ahead of time, make almost anything taste better, and can be kept in the fridge for at least several days. As for appetizers and desserts, we enjoy them, but don't regularly prepare homemade ones during the work week. Our usual weeknight sweet-tooth solution is to have ice cream and sprinkles always on hand.

For *Keepers* to be truly useful, though, we knew it needed to offer more than just stellar recipes. It needed to provide something that was missing from all the recipe search engines and chef smackdowns: moral support; strategies for planning your daily cooking; tips on how to season food, organize your pantry, and "fix" a dish; and advice at those crucial moments when you're stalled in the supermarket, staring blankly into your fridge, or flummoxed at the stove.

We also knew that it was important to hear what people wanted from such a cookbook—so that's exactly what we did. In planning *Keepers*, we spoke to dozens of family members, friends, friends of friends, and complete strangers whom we cornered in supermarket aisles to understand more fully the dilemmas of busy weeknight cooks. Here are some highlights of what we discovered:

NO GUILT! Turns out cookbooks can make you feel bad about your kitchen efforts, or lack thereof. We don't expect you to cook every night of the week; if you can manage to cook just a little more often than you already do, we think that's great.

ORGANIZE THE RECIPES BY MAIN INGREDIENT—FISH, CHICKEN, PORK, ETC.—NOT BY SEASON. That's how most of the people we talked to think about what they're going to prepare, so we obliged. We strongly believe in cooking with seasonal and local ingredients, though, so we suggest that you do your best to keep those factors in mind as you plan and shop.

NO SPECIALTY/EXOTIC/EXPENSIVE INGREDIENTS. When it comes to weeknight meals, people will immediately pass over a recipe that calls for any ingredient that isn't familiar and/or available at the supermarket, so we skipped things like preserved lemons and za'tar. Ditto break-the-bank ingredients like veal chops and chanterelle mushrooms.

There were also a couple suggestions that we chose *not* to follow. One was to include timing information. While this can be helpful in general, we didn't want you to be a slave to the clock wondering if you've done something wrong if you're still cooking 38 minutes into a 30-minute recipe. And what happens when your kid is bellowing for help with a multiplication problem or your chatty best friend calls? All of our recipes are geared toward weeknight cooking (e.g., no lengthy braising, no brunoising). Some take longer than others, but most should take less than 45 minutes.

The other suggestion concerned nutritional information. Not to downplay the importance of calorie counts and the like, but that's just not our focus here, nor our area of expertise. That said, we do keep an eye on the amount of butter we use in our everyday meals; cook with lots of "good" fats, vegetables, and grains; and steer clear of processed items. Also, there are no gimmicks or tricks, no hidden vegetable purees or ground chia seeds. This is real, honest food, made from scratch with fresh, wholesome ingredients and an emphasis on balance. And although the recipes were designed to be convenient and to please both adults and children, they are not dumbed down in any way.

Our goal in writing this book was to share the lessons we've learned over the past two decades to help you become a more efficient, confident, creative cook—to help you not only survive the Monday-to-Friday dinner rush with your sanity and kitchen intact but also have some fun along the way. It can be done (we swear), and *Keepers* will show you how.

Happy Cooking!

Caroline & Kathy

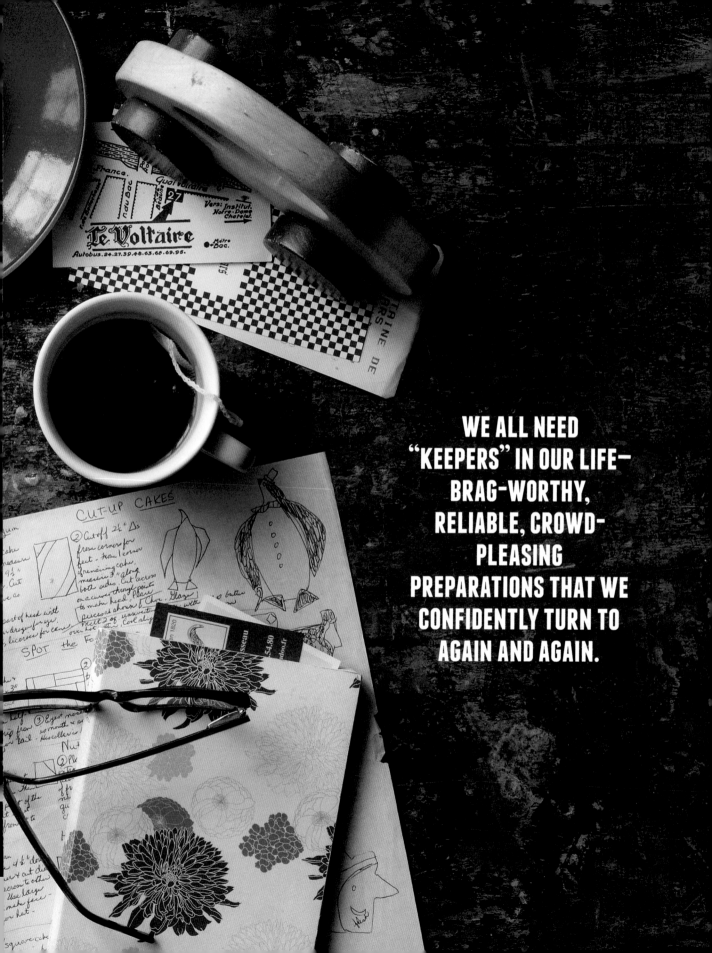

WE ALL NEED
"KEEPERS" IN OUR LIFE—
BRAG-WORTHY,
RELIABLE, CROWD-
PLEASING
PREPARATIONS THAT WE
CONFIDENTLY TURN TO
AGAIN AND AGAIN.

WHO WE ARE

Both of our moms were born in other countries and moved to the States in the early 1960s—Caroline's from Belgium, Kathy's from Japan. They also happened to be terrific cooks who married Irish-American men with a taste for meat and potatoes. This resulted in eclectic weekly childhood menus for each of us: In Caroline's house, *moules frites* and *céleri rémoulade* one night would be followed by pot roast the next; in Kathy's, miso soup and shrimp tempura would give way to ham and cabbage. Those dishes are still some of our favorites, but what we really took away from those meals was the devotion it took for our busy parents to put home-cooked food on the table almost every night (rare was the box of Hamburger Helper or potato chip–topped casserole, despite our pleas) and the pleasure of sitting down together at the end of the day.

Ever since we moved out on our own, cooking for ourselves, friends, and family has been important to both of us (some may even call it an obsession). The meals have evolved over the years—from giant omelets shared with ravenous roommates to braised short ribs for a lucky boyfriend to panko-crusted fish fingers that we hoped would coax a 5-year-old into eating something other than a carbohydrate—but the satisfaction we feel when cooking for others is always the same. (That's not to say we haven't had our share of kitchen disasters. Although growing up in food-minded families may have given us a head start at the stove, we've still torched some burgers along the way.)

Once we had kids, the desire to put our own food on the table became even greater, but so, too, did the challenges. Sometimes, trying to work dinner around chaotic schedules, finicky appetites, and general exhaustion makes us long for the simple days of Moo Goo Gai Pan eaten out of the carton on the couch. But we return to the kitchen night after night because sharing a home-cooked meal with those we love is one of the most fulfilling rituals we know.

HOW TO GET FROM MONDAY TO FRIDAY WITH YOUR SANITY—AND KITCHEN—INTACT

psych yourself up

There is a mom we know who is not what one might call a confident cook. About a year ago, she came by for a strong cup of tea and some gossip while the kids chased each other around the backyard. After the cups were emptied and the town scuttlebutt was exchanged, she looked at her watch and declared: "Well, time to go home and burn the dinner." And she wasn't kidding. She was already anticipating utter failure even before turning on the stove. Was this fatalism? Realism? Both?

We're the first to admit that cooking regularly—or more accurately, having to cook regularly—can be stressful and tedious. Even if you are someone who truly relishes cooking, there are likely days when you just want someone else to do it for you. Further complicating the issue is that cooking (particularly for those you love) isn't just a logistical feat—an equation involving time, ingredients, budgeting, skill, and desire. It's also an emotional endeavor. You, the cook, are putting yourself out there. You are making something that will feed and nourish someone. How will they react? Will they chew mutely? Tell you that this is the most delicious pot pie they've ever eaten? Admit that they prefer Grandma's version? Clean their plates and ask for seconds? Or say something like, "Tomorrow, let's just order in."

Maybe they don't know it, but you will be waiting for some kind of (hopefully positive, but at the very least constructive) response. None of us should underestimate the importance of complimenting, or simply acknowledging someone's cooking. Just knowing that their efforts were appreciated can be enough to inspire the most reluctant cook to keep at it. Even seasoned home cooks and professional chefs puff up from a rave review.

Our sense is that the aforementioned friend just needed some encouragement rather than a fire extinguisher. Maybe her doomsday attitude was the result of some unsuccessful or lackluster meals. Maybe she doubted her cooking abilities, or felt overwhelmed by the weeknight dinner rush. Sound familiar? We have since talked to many people who've admitted they have little faith in their cooking ability. For anyone who fits into this category, here's what we'd like you to know:

- **YOU ARE NOT ALONE.** Every night of the week, there are countless cooks who are stumped by planning a menu, feel challenged at the stove, or grow weary just thinking about getting dinner on the table. Take heart in the power of numbers.

- **WHEN YOU'RE THE COOK, YOU'RE THE BOSS.** Sure, you can prepare extra vegetables or a bigger salad for the vegetarian, or reserve some unsauced pasta for the picky eater, or leave the salmon off the plate of the fish hater, but don't turn into everyone's short-order cook.

- **START SIMPLY.** Before you tackle osso buco, work on a brag-worthy vinaigrette. Move on from there.

- **EVERYONE MESSES UP.** Keep calm, carry on, learn from your mistakes.

- **BREATHE.** When things get stressful in the kitchen, take a deep breath, ask for help when you need it, and pat yourself on the back no matter how the meal turns out.

- **BE THE COOK YOU WANT TO BE.** Just because you weren't tied to your grandmother's apron strings or were raised on frozen chicken nuggets doesn't mean it's too late to become an excellent home cook. Anyone who wants to do it, can. Just be determined, open-minded, and persistent.

- **FIND THE JOY.** Cooking should be fun, empowering even. Put on your favorite music, pour a glass of wine, admire how a sharp knife slices through a ripe tomato, savor the aroma of caramelizing onions, congratulate yourself on how evenly you seared the pork chops. When you start to enjoy the *process* of cooking, everything else gets easier, too.

planning

Aside from having a thoughtfully stocked pantry (see Shopping, page 4) and using reliable recipes, the other key to getting dinner on the table with minimal fuss and stress is to plan ahead. As one of our kids' teachers, a mom of two, said recently, "If I leave the house without any idea of what I'm cooking that night, it's all over." We couldn't agree more, which is why we kick ourselves whenever we find ourselves in 5 o'clock panic mode.

But even better is to think in terms of a week, not just a single night, and to do so before your big weekly shop. Choose Monday to Friday's meals based on what best fits everyone's schedule and the season. Also, consider the flow in terms of cooking times and technique so that one night you may be sautéing or stir-frying and the next assembling a hearty salad to serve with leftovers or a store-bought rotisserie chicken. Balance meat with fish and pasta, and one-dish meals with ones that consist of the more traditional protein, vegetable, and starch trio. Just try to give yourself one weeknight off a week: Have someone else cook—we have a rule that if you can ride a bike you can scramble an egg—order a pizza, make sandwiches, whatever.

TO HELP DECIDE YOUR MENUS, refer to the Recipes by Category (page 228), which lists mostly main courses under five headings: Extra-Fast, Popular with Kids, One-Dish Meals, Vegetarian, Staggered Dinner Times. After you choose your mains for the week, round them out with one or two side dishes, if needed. And unless you have the memory of an elephant, write down your week's menu, create your grocery shopping list accordingly, and keep the menu handy.

- IF MONDAY is a relatively calm day, make a double batch of something like Smoky Turkey Chili (page 64) or Lentil and Chorizo Soup (page 140) and serve the extra on an especially hectic day later in the week or freeze it for another week. (To save space and for faster thawing, use gallon-size resealable freezer bags. Label the bags, ladle in the chili, etc., squeeze out any excess air, then lay them flat in the freezer. When frozen, store them upright like books on a shelf. Portion out a few pint-size plastic containers for individual meals, too.)

- ON TUESDAY, if people will be eating at different times, make a dish that reheats well, such as Japanese-Style "Meat and Potatoes" (page 84), or that can be served at room temperature, such as Maple Barbecue Drumsticks (page 50).

- ON WEDNESDAY, if you have to work late or you know your energy will be flagging, pencil in a layup like Shrimp with Green Curry (page 23) or Penne with Broccoli Rabe, Garlic, and Crushed Red Pepper Flakes (page 114).

- THURSDAY might be a good night to put out all the odds and ends from the past few nights, maybe tacking on super-healthful Kale Salad with Pomegranate and Pumpkin Seeds (page 215).

- BY FRIDAY, a one-dish meal like Skillet Lasagna (page 129) or something more DIY like Turkey Tacos (page 65) eaten in front of a flick is sure to please.

ON SUNDAY, AFTER YOU'VE FIGURED OUT YOUR BASIC PLAN—knowing full well that you might need to make adjustments if your week gets topsy-turvy—and shopped for all the ingredients, take some time to get a head start on the week. It makes *a big* difference.

- For dinner that night, make a slow-cooking dish like a stew or roast that doesn't require much attention, but will likely yield leftovers, which are great for work lunches, too.
- Meanwhile, bang out one Lifesaver (pages 217–25), roast some vegetables (page 157), make a pot of black beans (page 188), grains (pages 197, 198, and 201), or rice, and wash and chop whatever vegetables you'll need for the next couple of meals.

With these items ready to go, you might even make it to Friday with energy to spare. Meal planning may seem daunting, but the more you do it, the easier it gets. And it's fine to repeat the same menu; just try to mix it up every once in a while so you, and the people you're feeding, don't get bored. How many of us grew up eating the same dinner on the same night each week? Baked chicken and green beans on Mondays, sloppy Joes on Wednesdays, fish 'n' chips on Fridays . . . If you can recite your weekly menu as readily as the Pledge of Allegiance, it's probably time to shake up the routine.

shopping

Our food shopping styles have changed dramatically since we moved to the suburbs and our schedules got busier. It may sound extreme, but we used to shop almost daily in New York City, and often at several specialty stores (the butcher shop, the fish market, the Asian grocer, etc.), for dinner provisions, basing the menu on what most appealed to us, looked the freshest, and that we could lug home without slipping a disk. Although we sometimes miss those neighborhood food runs, we have embraced shopping at the local mega-supermarket, ideally in one big weekly trip, and we rarely go without a list. Shopping hell is coming home after 2 hours and unloading 16 bags from the car only to realize you forgot to buy the milk. Here's what we've learned along the way:

KEEP A RUNNING, COMMUNAL SHOPPING LIST—AND REMEMBER TO BRING IT WITH YOU. Don't waste time at the end of the week trying to figure out what you need for your big shop. Keep a running list so you can just grab it and go whenever you head to the store. Better yet, have everyone in the household help maintain it; less work for you, and no one can blame you if you don't get something they can't live without. Keep a pad of paper and a Sharpie—also great for labeling freezer bags and jars (see Old Jars Are Good Jars, page 216)—near or attached to the fridge so as soon as anyone notices that something is running low or is out, they can jot it down. Those who haven't yet mastered the alphabet can draw a picture. Or, if you're the Excel sheet type, create a computerized list of staples organized by aisle, leaving space at the bottom of each section for write-in items. Print a bunch, pull one out each week, and have people circle or fill in what's needed. It may sound over the top if you've never done it, but it saves a lot of time and effort for very little work upfront. *And don't forget the list!* Of course, remembering the list doesn't ensure that it won't go MIA between the house and the store. Or does that only happen to us? Smartphone users have an easy fix: Take a photo of it.

EAT BEFORE YOU SHOP. When your blood sugar levels drop to dangerously low levels, items that normally never enter your cart suddenly become very appealing, things like Mallomars, Vienna sausages, and 5-pound bags of gummy bears. Caroline swears she blacked out from hunger once right after a big shop, only to come to in the car with a half-empty bag of sour cream and onion potato chips and jug of orange juice in her lap. So eat before walking through those sliding glass doors, even if it's just some trail mix downed in the parking lot. We've wised up and now keep a stash in the glove compartment.

GET TO KNOW YOUR LOCAL SUPERMARKET MANAGER. Not happy with the state of the romaine? Can't find wonton wrappers? Wonder why the supermarket 5 miles away sells cheaper organic milk? No sense in stewing about it; talk to someone. There's undoubtedly a store manager on call. Do you know his/her name? Find out. Ask questions and make your store work for you. In our experience, though, the bigger the store, the more proactive you have to be. The manager can answer questions about prices and availability, tell employees to pay closer attention to perishables, and might also special-order items for you. We've requested everything from farro to celeriac and coffee yogurt and now find them regularly.

GIVE YOUR SHOPPING CART A MAKEOVER. One comment that stuck with us while we were researching the book (i.e., making everyone we know talk to us about their weeknight meals situation in exchange for adult beverages) was from a mom of three who said: "I feel like every time I go to the supermarket I just end up buying the same 20 things: chicken breasts, broccoli, ground beef, lettuce, penne. . . . It's so boring, but I know what to do with those things, so I just get them again and again." We all have our "safeties"— ingredients that we can turn into a meal with our eyes closed—but when you find yourself making the same dishes every week (and we're betting on the same day), food boredom is inevitable.

The simplest way to break out of this rut is to go shopping with someone whose cooking style differs from yours. It can be fascinating to see what someone else buys— Swiss chard? parsnips? ground turkey?—and to learn what they do with them. "So, you make a pesto with the chard (page 123), roast the parsnips (page 157), and make chili with the turkey (page 64)?" And once you get comfortable expanding your choices, occasionally add a new ingredient to your cart, one that you would normally walk right by, and figure out a way to use it.

INGREDIENTS HAVE FRIENDS. If you're going to base your week of meals on one shop, it's important to be flexible with your ingredients, particularly the produce. Something may not be in stock, or it may not look fresh. So if your list says spinach, but the bunches at the store are limp, check out the Swiss chard. If it's glossy and vibrant, buy it. It may taste a little different and take a little longer to cook, but it's a great stand-in. Apply the same logic at home. If your recipe calls for sour cream but you only have Greek yogurt, use it. Keep in mind that the cooking times for each may vary. Here are some common substitutions:

Fresh tomato = grape or cherry tomatoes (Sun Golds are particularly good) = whole peeled canned tomato

Pork = turkey = chicken

Lamb = beef

Kale = Swiss chard = spinach

Broccoli = cauliflower

White potato = sweet potato

Root vegetable = any other root vegetable

Shallot = yellow onion

Chives = scallions

Any fresh herb = flat-leaf parsley

Lime = lemon

Crème fraîche = whole-milk Greek yogurt = sour cream

Mascarpone = cream cheese

Pancetta = bacon

Pine nuts = almonds = walnuts

Parmesan = pecorino = Grana Padano

White wine vinegar = distilled white vinegar = lemon juice

Maple syrup = honey = brown sugar

Fish sauce = anchovy paste

Panko = breadcrumbs

HUNT AND PECK. And don't be embarrassed about it. We're the first to admit we've toppled our share of apples looking for crisp, unbruised specimens. You should feel comfortable reaching past almost-expired egg or milk cartons, or asking for a fresher piece of fish or for your cold cuts to be sliced from a new piece of meat rather than the heel. There's no reason you should be assisting the store with the unloading of less-than-prime goods.

WATCH THE BOTTOM LINE. There are certain items that are going to lure you at the store: things like Himalayan pink salt, triple-crème washed-rind cheeses, and single-bean chocolate made by bearded guys in Brooklyn. You get the picture. These are tempting, but will inflate your bill so much that your spouse might frantically call you before you've even left the parking lot because he just received a credit card alert for an unusually high charge (true story). What's wrong with kosher salt, domestic cheddar, and Lindt bars, especially for everyday? If you want to indulge in such goodies, then we recommend the Web sites of some "gourmet" food stores (Murray's Cheese, Zingerman's, Kalustyan's) that specialize in them and generally sell them for less. Amazon is another option.

Another caveat is buying anything precut, precrumbled, prewashed, or already marinated. Not only does it cost more, it usually has a shorter shelf life. We do make two exceptions: precut butternut squash and ready-to-eat pomegranate seeds. The effort and mess saved at home is worth the markup.

Buying items like nuts, seeds, and granola in bulk is also a good way to save. But because it's hard to tell how long items have been sitting there, take a sample to test for freshness before filling your bag. Also, if a bulk item is unusually inexpensive, be skeptical. Apparently knock-offs aren't limited to just Louis Vuitton bags or Tide. We've heard tales of knock-off pine nuts, honey, and even extra-virgin olive oil.

PUT IT ALL AWAY. There's not much we can say to help you find room in the fridge for your groceries, but there are five things we (force ourselves to) do after our weekly shops that make the rest of the week that much easier:

1. Cajole a family member to return the empty bags (we use reusable ones as much as possible) back to the car so they're at the ready for the next trip.
2. Wash all the lettuce (see Everyday Salad Tip, page 207, for how to store it) and vegetables.
3. Rinse the herbs (except basil) and store them the same way as the lettuce.
4. Make a batch of a quick-cook grain like quinoa or bulgur for throwing into a soup or salad.
5. Boil six eggs. This last item may sound strange, but hard-boiled eggs always come in handy—for rounding out a meal, adding a little protein to a salad, or eating as an at-home or lunchbox snack.

shopping—with kids

If you're a parent, you understand why we devoted a separate section to this topic. Spilled Cheerios, sibling brawls, emergency bathroom sprints, meltdowns: There may be few things more dread-inducing than grocery shopping with young children (besides flying with them). We've experienced the good and the very bad and, over the years, figured out some strategies that markedly improve the odds of having a drama-free trip. And no, leaving the kids in the car is not one of them. . . .

CREATE YOUR OWN FOOD SAMPLES. Kids love when supermarkets have goodies to sample, even if it's something they don't normally care for, like bran muffins. Go figure. We love it, too, because not only does it satisfy their need to snack and keep the blood sugar levels stable, the mere act of munching provides a happy distraction. But not every store offers samples, at least not regularly (kudos to Whole Foods and Costco for being generous with them). So if hunger or a cranky period may coincide with a trip to the store, throw a couple beloved, easy-to-pack snacks—chocolate-covered raisins, for instance—in your bag before heading out the door. If you're unprepared and things are deteriorating fast, ask the person behind the deli counter for a slice of salami while he or she prepares your order. Or grab a bagel or tub of cubed watermelon. Is that wrong? Possibly. But desperate times call for desperate measures. Just don't forget to pay for the items at checkout. Otherwise, you're schooling your kids in the art of thievery.

MAKE A GAME OUT OF IT. The last thing you probably want us to tell you is that you should be prepared to entertain your kids at the supermarket. But when the witty banter runs out, injecting a little fun into the trip can actually help pass the time for all of you. You'll obviously have to adjust the "games" to the age level of your child/children, but here are some that our kids like:

- PLAY "I SPY" by telling them a few items on your list and asking them to find them as you stroll the aisles. The memory game is another favorite. See if they can remember what aisle number certain items are in.

- ASK THEM WHAT DISH they would create if you gave them x, y, and z and have them talk you through their recipe.

- HAVE THEM SELECT AND BAG some of the produce, and be specific with your requests so you're also teaching them what to look for: apples with no bruises, "heavy, fragrant" lemons, a pineapple that smells "sweet, but not strong" at the stem end, cauliflower that is "creamy white."

- JOIN THEM IN GUESSING how much a bunch of bananas, etc., weighs and then let them weigh it, which is a good opportunity to teach them how to read a scale. The person with the closest guess "wins."

- SIMILARLY, HAVE THEM GUESS how much the bill will be as you approach the cashier. As they get older, this will become an eye-opening experience.

GET THEM BAGGING EARLY. Once, Caroline noticed a mom in the next check-out line bagging an epic amount of groceries while her tween slouched nearby, immersed in a hand-held video game. Resisting the desire to swat the boy with a loaf of bread, she could only wonder why his mom wasn't telling him to help her. In addition to saving you time at the store, the good part about enlisting your kids' assistance at a young age with bagging—not to mention the actual shopping—is that they'll probably think it's fun and relish being trusted with a "big person's" job. Meanwhile, you're helping them develop life skills. ("Put the heavy stuff on the bottom and the cold items together." "Don't put the eggs under the jug of orange juice." "Be sure not to overload the bags.")

10 FLAVOR-BOOSTING PANTRY STAPLES

Our pantries are our war chests. Our individual stashes vary, but generally include a few different oils, vinegars, pastas, and grains; canned tuna and tomatoes; Thai curry paste; chicken broth; panko; beans, both canned and dried; spices and dried herbs; and coconut milk. Along with a few freezer basics—frozen peas (also good for treating injuries), quick-thawing chicken tenders and shrimp, garlic cubes (see The Many Faces of Garlic, page 154), a knob of ginger (it freezes well and there's no need to thaw it before grating), shredded cheddar, tortillas, and pizza dough—these supplies guarantee that whether we're faced with a bare refrigerator, a pack of turkey cutlets that's unexpectedly gone bad, or a burned pot of chili (don't ask), we'll be able to make a decent dinner without a last-minute run to the store.

But we have a second set of staples that are equally important. We call them our flavor boosters, and rely on them when a touch of heat, sweetness, brightness, acidity, umami, tang, richness, or crunch is needed. These ingredients aren't always noted in our recipes because using them is often a matter of personal taste and of what a particular dish might need at that particular moment to get it to taste its best. Here are the 10 we reach for most, at the start of preparing a dish, the middle, or right before we serve it:

1
ANCHOVY PASTE

Even if you don't like anchovies, you might like the deep, savory flavor anchovy paste contributes to a dish. (Once it's incorporated, there's no discernible fishiness.) It's quite versatile—stir it into tomato sauces, dressings, meat rubs, soups, stews, and braises—but also pretty potent, so use it sparingly. The paste usually comes in convenient tubes that can be recapped and kept in the refrigerator for about a year.

2
APPLE CIDER VINEGAR

Inexpensive and widely available, this is a great basic vinegar that pairs particularly well with meats, sauces, soups, and salads that are "apple friendly"; think pork or chicken, cream-based sauces, root vegetable soups, and green salads with sharp cheeses or dried fruits. Just a splash is needed to lend a mellow, apple-tinged note and heighten the flavors in a dish.

3
MISO PASTE

This nutritious Japanese fermented staple, most commonly made with soy beans, is good for far more than soup. The two main types are shiro (white) and aka (red), but miso ranges from light-colored, sweet, and mild to dark, savory, and robust. We find the light ones more versatile and use them to add depth and intensity to dressings, dips, marinades, compound butters, stews, and, yes, soups. Miso is popping up in more stores (avoid brands with MSG or preservatives) and keeps practically forever.

4
CITRUS JUICES AND ZESTS

A few drops of fresh lemon, lime, or orange juice can brighten just about any flat-tasting dish. But don't overlook the outside of the fruit. Most of our citrus skins go into the trash "naked" because we've stripped them of their highly aromatic and flavorful zest. It's perfect for lending a citrusy note to a dressing, compound butter, sauce, grain dish, meat or fish rub, braise, etc. in a dry, concentrated form. This is particularly useful if the preparation includes dairy, which may curdle from the acid in the juice. If the dish already includes lemon, lime, or orange juice, though, you can still add the zest: The layering of flavors will make it even better.

5
CRUSHED RED PEPPER FLAKES

When a dish needs a little kick, look to crushed red pepper flakes. It's our standard heat source for everything from pasta sauces and marinades to soups and stir-fries. When possible, include it at the start of a dish, as part of the flavor base, so its warmth can spread during cooking. There's no need to buy fancy pepper flakes; the simple supermarket variety is fine.

6
FLAT-LEAF PARSLEY

Think of fresh Italian parsley (not the curly variety) as far more than just a decorative garnish. A generous handful thrown into most dishes just before serving adds vibrant color and a refreshing, grassy bite. It can also be a main ingredient in salads and grain dishes or turned into a simple, lively "sauce" for meat, fish, or potatoes when combined with some minced garlic, lemon juice and/or zest, and good olive oil. You could also embellish the sauce with some chopped capers, olives, red onion, hard-boiled egg, or anchovy fillets—paste would work, too. However you use it, resist the temptation to chop it to dust. It's much more interesting when roughly chopped or even torn.

7
GREEK YOGURT

Trendiness and cost aside, there's nothing not to love about tart, thick Greek yogurt, which is available in almost every supermarket these days. It's commonly eaten drizzled with honey or dolloped over fruit or granola, but it's great in savory preparations, too. It lends tangy creaminess and body to sauces, dips, soups, and stews, and in marinades, it tenderizes and flavors. The whole-milk variety adds more richness and flavor than those with less fat, but we'll leave that call to you.

8
MAPLE SYRUP

The real stuff is expensive, but a little goes a long way. It adds a sweet, caramel-y note to dressings and marinades and can also be used to balance a dish that is too acidic. And unlike sugar or brown sugar, there aren't any granules that need to be dissolved. It may be counterintuitive, but choose Grade B over Grade A for its richer maple flavor.

9
TOASTED SEEDS

When chefs create a dish, they're always thinking about the interplay of textures. One-dimensional dishes can get boring pretty fast, no matter how delicious they are. Nuts are a classic choice for adding crunch, but since they can be pricey and so many people have nut allergies, we're using seeds more and more. Pumpkin, sesame, and sunflower seeds are versatile, economical, and healthful favorites and are even better when toasted. If they're not pretoasted (sometimes labeled "roasted"), put them in a single layer in a heavy skillet over medium heat and toss often until fragrant and golden, 2 to 4 minutes, or bake on a sheet pan at 350°F for 5 to 10 minutes, tossing once or twice; use the same processes for toasting nuts. Add them to salads, sauces, pestos (in place of nuts), vegetables, and soups. We generally store seeds and nuts in the freezer so they stay fresher longer.

10
TOMATO PASTE

Lots of preparations benefit from the pop, intensity, and body a spoonful of tomato paste provides: tomato or pizza sauces, fish-, meat-, or vegetable-based soups, stews, braises. We prefer the tubed variety to canned. Once opened, it stays fresh in the fridge for months (the canned version always goes bad before we finish it), it has a brighter tomato flavor, and there's none of the characteristic "tinny-ness" of canned foods. Tubed paste tends to be more concentrated, so use it accordingly.

organizing the kitchen

Every kitchen is different. Every kitchen is personal. And a kitchen doesn't need to be fancy or space-aged to be functional. Take the great Julia Child's famed Cambridge kitchen, with the pegboard her husband created for her pots and pans, each lovingly outlined. This efficient workspace was put in the Smithsonian not because Julia had marble countertops and a stove that can boil water in 60 seconds. She didn't. It's famous because it was hers, but it warranted preservation because it shows that great things can come from cleverly orchestrated yet humble environments.

Aside from our professional-style ranges, our own kitchens leave a lot to be desired: think limited work and storage space, low-hanging cabinets (our stand mixers and blenders can't fit under them and we bump our heads on them when we lean over our cutting boards), lots of Formica. But we make them work as effectively as possible by focusing on the organization—and keeping them organized. You've probably heard some of these tips before, but they bear repeating because often just a few minor changes can make any kitchen function better. Of course, if something works for you, stick with it.

SALT SHOULD BE THE MOST ACCESSIBLE INGREDIENT IN YOUR KITCHEN. Keep your salt handy in an open dish; you can cover it when you're not cooking. We put ours between the stove and main prep area, which are right next to each other. If these two spaces are more than a step apart, leave a dish at each area. An open dish lets you readily dip in a measuring spoon or, better yet, when preparing savory dishes, your fingers to grab a pinch. And the more you use your fingers, the more you will develop a "feel" for how much salt you need to take to season something. If you like to sprinkle a finishing salt like fleur de sel on foods before serving them, keep that nearby in a dish, too.

KEEP YOUR OILS AND VINEGARS NEAR THE STOVE. Not too close, because the heat could cause them to deteriorate, but no more than a step away. If you don't like clutter on your countertop, put them in the closest cabinet. Either way, make sure the good stuff is visible: Just catching a glimpse of the lovely walnut oil or aged balsamic you splurged on can inspire you to use it.

STORE FREQUENTLY REACHED-FOR ITEMS IN CLEAR, SEALABLE CONTAINERS. Transfer flour, sugar, rice, fruit leathers, granola bars, etc., to big jars set on the counter or in the pantry. It's easier to access them (no fumbling with a rumpled bag or ripped open box) and they tend to stay fresher longer. You can also see at a glance when you're running low on something.

DIVIDE THE SPICES. If space is tight, keep only the ones you use often at arm's reach. Put the rest in a plastic bin (write the name of the spice on the top of the jar for easy identification) elsewhere in the kitchen. One creative storage solution is to hang a plastic shoe holder bag on the back of a pantry door and slide a few jars into each see-through pouch. Also, date the jars when you open them; spices generally have a 1-year shelf life. If it's relatively odorless, it's relatively tasteless.

GROUP INGREDIENTS AND EQUIPMENT BY HOW YOU USE THEM. If you love to bake, keep baking-related items—cake flour, vanilla extract, confectioners' sugar, muffin pans, whisks, pastry brushes, candy thermometers, etc.—together, preferably in one area. Apply the same logic to nonperishables specific to different cuisines. That way, when you make an Indian curry from scratch, for instance, you don't have to hunt for the ground turmeric or fennel seeds. Unless you frequently cook with those items, consider storing them in individual plastic bins (marked Indian, Japanese, etc.) and housing them where space isn't at a premium.

IF YOU HAVE KIDS, SET UP AN ACCESSIBLE "KID-APPROVED" ZONE. This can be a shelf, a drawer, or a section on the counter. Use it to hold snacks and, if the kids are young and like to cook alongside you, an assortment of kid-friendly cookware, dishware, etc. That way, they can help themselves and it's clear what they can and can't eat or use.

HOUSE CUTTING BOARDS AT ARM'S REACH. If you have to take more than one step from your prep area to get a cutting board—we recommend having two large and two small; more if you like help in the kitchen—relocate them. Ditto knives, measuring cups and spoons, and mixing bowls.

INSTEAD OF STACKING, STORE VERTICALLY. It's annoying to wrestle with a pile of baking, roasting, and sheet pans in a cabinet to get the one you want, which is inevitably stuck somewhere in the middle. Vertical holders are nice, but not necessary: Just prop the pans upright on their sides. The same goes for cutting boards and platters. They're much easier to take out and put away this way. Avoid stacking your most frequently used pots and sauté pans, too. Hang them from a rack or at least keep them at the front of a stove-side cabinet and on the top of the pile, even if they're bigger than the other vessels.

HAVE A STACK OF DISH TOWELS HANDY. They don't have to be fancy; any old large rectangle of cotton cloth can be used to wipe down a counter, dry blanched vegetables, cover rising dough, or fill in as an apron. And they're much more economical than paper towels, but since paper towels are likely as much a part of your household as they are ours . . .

GET A PAPER TOWEL HOLDER THAT WORKS WITH ONE HAND. Sounds trivial, until both of your hands are dirty or you're holding something in one, say, a slippery phone, chicken, or child.

IF YOU HAVEN'T USED IT IN A YEAR, FIND A NEW HOME FOR IT. Are you really going to use that dusty pasta maker you received as a wedding present 15 years ago? And think twice about that melon baller, too. Even though it doesn't take up much space, you still have to store it and root past it to find other items you do use. Be ruthless; later, you'll wonder what took you so long.

10 KITCHEN TOOLS WORTH THE SPACE

We're not big on gadgets or gizmos, but certain tools make our time in the kitchen more efficient, safer, and even more enjoyable. We could live without them, but we wouldn't want to.

1
BENCH SCRAPER

Also called a pastry scraper, this handy tool gets so much use in our kitchens it sometimes feels like an extension of our hands. It's indispensable, not just when making doughs and scraping up the remnants from the counter, but can also be used for crushing, chopping, and cutting (once you cut brownies with it, you'll never go back to a knife). And it's ideal for quickly and cleanly scooping up ingredients from the cutting board (support them on the blade with your free hand). Though you can buy plastic versions for a couple dollars with a flexible, curved edge that's perfect for scraping bowls clean, for chopping, a stronger, sharper metal-edged one is needed. Some models also include convenient ruler markings.

2
BENRINER SLICER

Forget bulky, heavy, costly French mandolines. For a fraction of the size, heft, and price, the Japanese Benriner slicer is all you need to slice and julienne even the hardest vegetables in seconds. We also prefer it to a food processor for those tasks—unless large quantities are involved—because the slicer is more accessible and easier to clean. Just be sure to use the safety guard—the blade is SHARP.

3
COPPER GRATIN DISHES

These shallow, oval vessels are so handsome and evocative (think Parisian brasseries), we'd probably use them even if they weren't so functional. They can go from refrigerator to oven/stove to table; transfer heat quickly and cool down rapidly; promote even cooking and browning; and handle roast chicken, eggplant Parmesan, pan-roasted pork tenderloin, vegetable gratins, and fruit crisps with equal aplomb. The one downside is the price, so look for them on sale or at secondhand stores. They come in different sizes and finishes—we find the 13 x 9-inch stainless steel–lined model to be the most practical—but whichever you buy will last a lifetime.

4
FISH SPATULA

We first discovered this thin, flexible, slotted, and tapered spatula while working in restaurant kitchens. Its design makes it easy to slide under the most delicate fish without breaking it, and it doesn't scoop up any extra cooking oil or other pan liquid in the process. But it's also great for eggs and cookies and sturdy enough to handle burgers and other heavy items, or potentially sticky ones, such as roasted vegetables; in fact, the "fish" spatula is now the main spatula we use.

5
QUALITY TONGS

There so many bad tongs out there—and why does every house seemingly have a pair? Some don't grip food securely or pierce it; others are flimsy, won't lock shut, and/or have springs that are so loose they barely open at all. The basic stainless-steel variety made by Edlund is our favorite. There are fancier, pricier tongs, but they aren't more functional or durable. Stock your kitchen with the 9- and 12-inch sizes and use them without issue for grilling, broiling, sautéing, roasting, boiling, even stirring in a pinch.

6
KITCHEN SHEARS

Cut herbs such as parsley, cilantro, and chives with these sharp, sturdy scissors rather than chopping them with a knife. This method works for scallions, too. Large pieces of herbs are just more interesting flavor- and texture-wise—so we rarely mince them anyway. It's fast, easy, doesn't require a cutting board, and can be done right over the pot, pan, bowl, or plate. Kitchen shears are also great for cutting bacon and dried fruit (unless you're working with large quantities), separating chicken parts at the joints, cutting pizza slices, and trimming pie dough.

7
HALF SHEET PANS

With their wide surface area and low sides, these pans (roughly 18 x 13 inches) are ideal for making granola, roasted potatoes and vegetables, jelly rolls, cookies, and baked fish or cutlets, as well as for toasting nuts, seeds, coconut, and breadcrumbs. We also line them with foil and put them in the oven under sputtery, leaky dishes like lasagna and pies; fit them with a rack to catch crumbs from cooling cakes or cookies; and line them with paper bags for draining fried foods. They're great as trays, too. One pan is good, but if you cook often or for a crowd, two or more is better. Don't skimp on quality here, though. You don't want them to warp or buckle or have jagged, unfinished edges. Restaurant supply shops sell them for less than $10 or so.

8
QUART-SIZE MEASURING CUP

Since this vessel can accommodate any amount from 1 to 4 cups, sometimes it's the only measurer you'll need for a recipe (see Crustless Broccoli and Cheddar Quiche, page 103). Not only is it much more efficient to measure 4 cups of liquid in one go than twice in a 2-cup vessel, you can measure several ingredients that will be cooked together—say, 1 cup each of onions, carrots, and celery—by adding them on top of one another, then dump them into the pot or pan all at once.

9
SMOOTH-EDGE CAN OPENER

After one-too-many cut fingers from jagged-edged lids, we switched to smooth-edge can openers. Bonus: no more fishing the lid out of the can since these openers remove it in such a way that it's too big to fall in.

10
THIN, CHEAP, BIG POT

Heavy-bottomed, sturdy pots and pans, which distribute and hold heat evenly, are unbeatable for searing, slow cooking aromatics, and braising, but when it comes to cooking pasta or blanching vegetables, nothing beats thin, cheap cookware of the lobster pot variety. Our mothers and grandmothers actually used nothing but—and still managed to make the best food. In them, water comes to a boil fast, and after you add the ingredients, returns to the boil quickly, exactly what you need to prevent soggy noodles and waterlogged, dull-looking green beans and such.

cooking

After years of hanging out in kitchens with family and friends, we're convinced that most people are just a move or two away from becoming much better cooks. These tips, which anyone can adopt immediately, will help you avoid some of the most common culinary missteps and can mean the difference between so-so and really good food, not to mention safer, less harried cooking.

LOOK THE PART. Making brownies with the kids or a leisurely stew on the weekend is one thing, but when you're cooking against the clock, form really affects function. Here's our basic checklist: **hair back** to prevent stray strands from falling into the polenta or blocking your view (particularly problematic when chopping); **shoes on** (as anyone who has ever had a knife fall on their foot can attest, flip-flops and ballet flats don't count); **dishtowel tucked into waistband** from one corner at the ready for wiping hands, knife, plate edges, or work area (chefs are never without their side towel for a reason); **flammable peasant blouse off,** tighter-fitting (and washable) shirt on; and **sleeves short or rolled up** (the gravy belongs in the pan, not on your cuffs). Also, try to **stand with your legs about shoulder width apart,** your **weight equally on both feet,** your **back straight,** and **shoulders back**. You'll have better balance and endurance.

SET THE TABLE AND POUR THE DRINKS BEFORE YOU TURN ON THE STOVE. Unless you're preparing just one dish with more than 10 minutes of lag time, it's better to get this out of the way first. We always think we'll have time to do it before dinner is ready, but there are invariably distractions—the doorbell will ring, the dog will need to go out, one of the kids will send you an *urgent* text—and then we're scrambling at the table while the food gets cold and everyone's hungry. Of course, if someone can do those tasks for you, take advantage.

BE YOUR OWN SOUS CHEF. Prepping and cooking at the same time can be a recipe for disaster (pun intended), so here's what we recommend: If you're making a new dish, read the entire recipe a couple times before you start cooking to make sure you have all the ingredients and understand the process (there's nothing like getting halfway through a recipe only to find out the meat needs to marinate overnight). Set a large cutting board on top of a flat damp dishcloth or paper towel to keep it from slipping, and work next to the sink if possible so you can easily scrape in trimmings and rinse your knife. Gather and measure or chop all the ingredients before turning on the stove to economize your movements and ensure you're not playing catch-up while the oil overheats. Lastly, clean as you go. Even if you only put the dirty bowls and utensils in the sink when you're done with them, it will keep your work area neater and make the task of cleaning up less daunting. And dinner's more enjoyable when you know there's not a big mess waiting for you in the kitchen.

LET INGREDIENTS LOSE THEIR CHILL BEFORE COOKING THEM. This isn't as much of an issue with longer, slower cooking methods like braising and poaching, but when grilling, sautéing, frying, or stir-frying, foods at or close to room temperature generally cook more evenly, not to mention faster. Get in the habit of setting meats, fish, and refrigerated vegetables on the counter at least 20 minutes before preparing them (no more for fish, though). If you have to start cooking as soon as you get home, just leave them out for as long as you can.

TOUCH YOUR FOOD—WITH YOUR HANDS! Not long ago, while watching a cookbook author prepare a roasted chicken on a morning television show, we were struck by the fact that she put salt, lemon juice, and olive oil on the bird without actually touching it. Perhaps she didn't want to mingle with raw poultry juices so early in the day (her outfit was pretty), but primly depositing those essential ingredients on a few areas and foregoing contact seemed unsporting. Pretty much any food will taste better if the seasonings are rubbed into every nook and cranny, and often your hands are the best tools for the job. Hands are also the gentlest way to toss a salad and transfer raw meats and fish from the counter to the pan. And with a little practice, a couple pokes with your index finger can tell you when the latter are rare (the flesh will feel soft, squishy), medium (it will have some give), or well done (it will be quite firm). Keep in mind that the residual heat will cook the item a little more as it rests— see below for more on this—so remove it from the heat a little before it is done to your liking. When in doubt, though, err on the side of caution; you can always cook the item longer.

COOK AT A HIGHER TEMPERATURE THAN YOU MIGHT THINK WHEN SAUTÉING OR SEARING. Heat is what creates a crisp exterior, seals in the juices, and leaves caramelized bits in the bottom of the pan that you can use to make a flavorful pan sauce. If the temperature is too low, the ingredients will steam and stick instead and will likely be tough and/or turn an unappealing color.

LET FOOD REST BEFORE SERVING IT. This mainly applies to things like quick-cooked meats or roasts. The residual heat will finish cooking the meat (allow about 10 minutes for a steak and 15 to 20 for a roast; the degree of doneness may rise half a level or so). The rest time also allows the juices to redistribute so they don't run out as readily when the meat is cut. That said, lasagna and pot pie are also easier to serve when they've firmed up a bit, and foods like chili and soups tend to improve after the flavors have melded for a day or so.

DON'T BE AFRAID TO USE SALT AND BUTTER. Chefs use salt and butter liberally, which is why restaurant food is (generally) so flavorful. That's not to say that you should overload your food with them, especially if you have dietary restrictions. But you will definitely taste the difference when, for instance, you generously salt the water for vegetables and pastas; finish a sauce with a knob of butter; or baste a piece of meat or fish with some butter melted into the pan juices and then sprinkle it with some salt—maybe a finishing salt, such as fleur de sel—before serving.

DEGREASE YOUR PAN. Whether you've sautéed a piece of fish or roasted a turkey, if you're going to make a sauce/gravy in the same pan, take a few seconds to tilt the pan and skim off the fat with a spoon before you proceed (if you're going to include aromatics like garlic or shallots, leave 1 or 2 tablespoons). A layer of oil floating on the surface of even the most delicious sauce/gravy is just plain gross—to look at and eat.

TASTE, TASTE, TASTE. We can't emphasize this enough. Taste as you cook and definitely taste before you serve a dish. As you do, ask yourself: Does it need more salt to emphasize flavors that may have faded during cooking? Some acid—a squeeze of lemon juice or splash of vinegar—to brighten it? Some pepper for kick? A pinch of sugar or honey to balance any tartness? Or a drizzle of olive oil to give it a little richness? Make the adjustments, then taste again, and again—and again, if needed. A dish isn't done when you've completed the recipe; it's done when it tastes right.

SPEND A MINUTE ON PRESENTATION. Even if it's a Wednesday night and you're serving leftover stew, pay a little attention to how you plate your food. We know there will be (many!) nights when it's all you can do to just get a home-cooked meal on the table, but even a gesture as simple as twisting pasta into a mound (see photo, below, and Tip, page 112), leaning a pork chop against a pile of couscous, sprinkling some chopped parsley on buttered green beans, or nestling lime wedges around a platter of grilled shrimp will make the food look even more appetizing and will make everyone, including you, feel special.

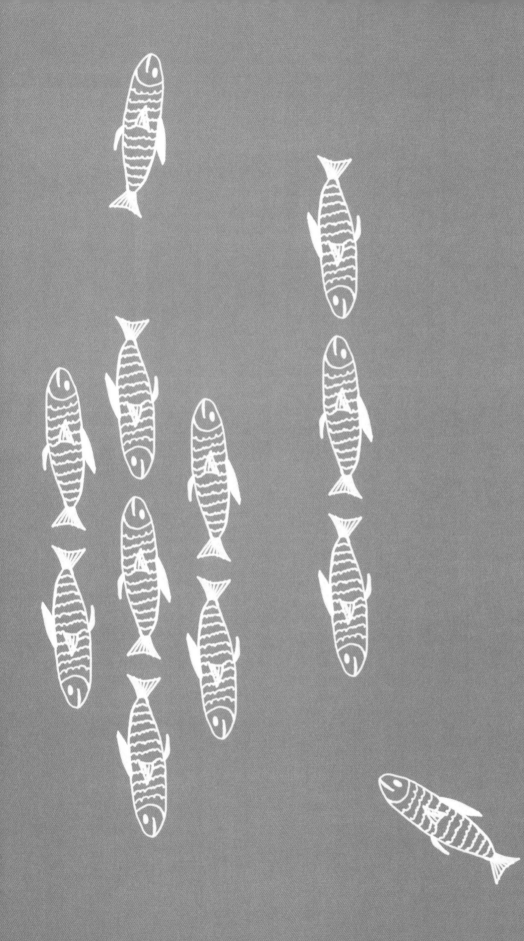

FISH AND SHELLFISH

ROASTED ORANGE CHIPOTLE SHRIMP

SERVES 4

Roasting is a great way to cook shrimp: It intensifies their flavor and leaves them tender and succulent. It's simple, too. Just season, then put them in the oven. Roasted shrimp can be eaten hot or cold and paired with a variety of sauces, including traditional cocktail sauce. We like to toss them with this slightly sweet, spicy, smoky orange chipotle sauce. Serve the combination over your favorite rice or grain or wrapped inside a warm flour tortilla with lettuce and maybe some crumbled goat cheese.

1½ pounds large shrimp, peeled and deveined

1 tablespoon olive oil, plus 2 tablespoons

Salt and pepper

2 garlic cloves, minced, then smeared into a paste

1 chipotle chile in adobo sauce (remove the seeds for a milder effect), minced, then smeared into a paste

2 tablespoons apple cider vinegar

2 tablespoons orange juice

1 teaspoon honey

Dash of Worcestershire sauce

2 scallions (white and pale green parts only), thinly sliced on the diagonal

—Preheat the oven to 400°F, with a rack in the upper third position. Put the shrimp on a sheet pan (lined with foil for easier cleanup, if you like), add the 1 tablespoon oil, season with salt and pepper, and toss to combine. Spread the shrimp out in a single layer, then roast until almost cooked through, about 6 minutes. Let rest for a few minutes. (Shrimp get rubbery when overcooked, so it's better to remove them from the heat a little early and let the residual heat finish cooking them. You can always return them to the heat for another minute or two if you find them too rare.)

—Meanwhile, make the orange chipotle sauce. In a large bowl, whisk together the garlic, chipotle, vinegar, orange juice, honey, Worcestershire sauce, and the remaining 2 tablespoons oil. Check the seasonings.

—Add the shrimp and scallions to the sauce and toss to combine. Check the seasonings and serve.

TIP: Chipotle chiles/peppers (smoked jalapeños) in adobo—a mixture of tomatoes, vinegar, spices, and garlic—are generally found canned in the Mexican section of the supermarket. They lend a unique bite of heat and a mellow smokiness. One small can contains about 6 chiles, so store the rest in an airtight container in the refrigerator, where they should last for months. The Smoky Turkey Chili on page 64 and the Black Bean and Butternut Squash Enchiladas on page 104 also use the chiles.

SAME RESULT, DIFFERENT PROCESS

Want to know how to make a dish turn out the same each time? Cook it differently each time. Think about it. The taste, texture, size, and quality of ingredients vary: Carrots can be sweet or slightly bitter; apples crisp or soft; chicken legs fat or skinny, scallops dry or watery. So in order to get the same result, you have to see what you're dealing with and then adjust the way you handle the item—and the dish—accordingly.

Like many things, we learned this the hard way. Here's one memorable example: Kathy once made a scallop pasta that she'd prepared a dozen times before without issue. But this time, when the diced scallops hit the hot pan slicked with olive oil, garlic, and red pepper flakes, they immediately started oozing liquid instead of searing. She froze and kept watching them bubble away, getting progressively tougher while the pasta on the next burner overcooked. Then she started kvetching: "Dinner's ruined, those scallops were crazy expensive, I'm calling the fish store...." And she ended up serving soggy noodles with rubbery scallops in a watery sauce.

Once she'd calmed down, she thought about how she could have salvaged the dish:

— Quickly removed the scallops from the pan, patted them dry, and cooked them in another, searing-hot, dry pan.

— Reduced the scallop liquid in the first pan to a tasty sauce, perhaps swirling in some butter to make it even richer.

— Not ignored the pasta. But she was too focused on the fact that the dish wasn't turning out the way it usually does.

The upshot? Cook the ingredients, not the recipe. That may be easier said than done, but the first step to doing it is knowing it. Ruining dinner helps, too.

SHRIMP WITH GREEN CURRY

SERVES 4

This dish always seems to get a "wow" when we serve it. It also takes less than 15 minutes to make, thanks to jarred Thai green curry paste, which is one of our pantry staples. Yes, fresh curry paste is superior, but we can't always find lemongrass, Thai ginger, kaffir lime, and bird's eye chiles, and grinding them is a whole 'nother story. Recommended brands include Mae Ploy and Maesri. Feel free to substitute different vegetables, such as thinly sliced carrots, sugar snaps, or frozen peas, in place of the green beans.

—In a large skillet, heat the oil over medium heat. Add the curry paste and anchovy paste and cook, stirring constantly, until fragrant, about 30 seconds. Add the coconut milk and brown sugar and stir to combine. Simmer, stirring occasionally, until the sauce thickens slightly, about 3 minutes.

—Add the shrimp and green beans and simmer, stirring occasionally, until the shrimp are almost cooked through, 2 to 3 minutes. (Shrimp get rubbery when overcooked, so it's better to remove them from the heat a little early and let the residual heat finish cooking them. You can always return them to the heat for another minute or two if you find them too rare.)

—Stir in the scallions and a generous squeeze of lime juice, then check the seasonings. (If the curry and anchovy pastes didn't provide enough salt, add some.) Serve the curry with steamed rice, Sriracha, and/or cilantro, if you like.

1/2 tablespoon vegetable oil

2 tablespoons jarred Thai green curry paste

1 teaspoon anchovy paste

One 13.5-ounce can unsweetened coconut milk

1 tablespoon dark brown sugar

1 pound large shrimp, peeled, deveined, and cut into bite-size pieces

1/2 pound green beans, cut on the diagonal into bite-size pieces

2 scallions, sliced on the diagonal

Fresh lime juice

Steamed rice

Sriracha or hot sauce of your choice (optional)

Handful of cilantro, roughly chopped (optional)

MUSSELS THE BELGIAN WAY

SERVES 4

Both of us were fortunate to have kitchen "mentors" growing up—someone who passed down not just basic kitchen know-how, but also a sense of delight and command at the stove. For Kathy, it was her Japanese mother, who was blessed with a can-do attitude, spot-on palate, and amazing knife skills (her mantra: "It's not the knife, but the way you use it"); for Caroline, it was her Belgian grandmother, a petite but mighty woman who, wearing heels and an apron, prepared everything from rich rabbit stews to bright currant sorbets in her tiny Brussels kitchen. Known as "Mamy" by everyone, she taught not by lecturing or handing over the whisk, but by just doing her thing. That's how Caroline learned how to make these classic mussels. (Beer is involved, but not much, and some of the alcohol cooks away, leaving a subtle earthy flavor.)

Mamy served her moules with crispy frites that everyone dipped in mayonnaise. Caroline's weeknight alternative is to make buttery garlic toasts to sop up the tasty broth. If you want to serve fries, though, you can always pick some up at the closest burger joint. Even the Belges do this—but never Mamy.

4 tablespoons unsalted butter, softened, plus 2 tablespoons

2 garlic cloves, minced

16 baguette slices, $\frac{1}{2}$ inch thick and cut on the diagonal

2 shallots, minced

2 celery stalks, thinly sliced

Salt and pepper

4 pounds mussels, scrubbed and debearded, if needed (discard any mussels with gaping or cracked shells)

$\frac{3}{4}$ cup beer, preferably a pale lager, such as Stella Artois

Large handful of flat-leaf parsley, chopped

$\frac{1}{4}$ cup heavy cream

—Preheat the oven to 350°F, with a rack in the middle position. In a small bowl, mash together the 4 tablespoons butter and garlic. Put the bread in a single layer on a sheet pan fitted with a wire rack, spread the garlic butter on top of the slices, and bake until golden brown and crispy, about 10 minutes. (If the garlic bread is ready before the mussels, wrap in foil to keep warm.)

—Meanwhile, in a large pot with a lid, melt the remaining 2 tablespoons butter over medium-low heat. Add the shallots and celery, season with salt and pepper, and cook, stirring occasionally, until softened, about 6 minutes.

—Add the mussels and beer, cover the pot, raise the heat to medium-high, and bring the liquid to a boil. Cook for 2 minutes, then shake the pot by quickly jerking it upward and toward you, almost like you're jumping rope backward. This will move the mussels from the bottom of the pot to the top so they cook evenly. Repeat several times. (You don't want to stir them because removing the lid would let out the steam that gently cooks them.) It might take a little practice before it feels comfortable, but if Caroline's 90-pound grandmother could do it, so can you.

—Cook the mussels for 2 minutes more, then crack open the lid. If at least three-fourths of the mussels have opened, add the parsley and cream, replace the lid, and shake the pot a couple more times to combine. Check the broth seasonings. Serve the mussels and broth in individual bowls or in one big bowl for sharing, with the garlic bread on the side or in the bowls. Discard any mussels that haven't opened. Putting a bowl on the table for empty shells is helpful.

POACHED FILLETS OF THE DAY WITH LEMON BUTTER SAUCE

SERVES 4

For anyone with a fear of cooking fish (we've certainly dealt with our share of bone-dry fillets), this recipe is for you. Poaching is a very forgiving way of preparing fish: It won't burn or overcook if you step away for a minute; it won't stick to the pan; and you don't even have to flip it. This traditional French preparation might seem arcane, but the results are pretty impressive considering you do little more than put a handful of ingredients in a pan, throw it in the oven for a few minutes, then whisk in some butter and lemon juice. (You can also poach on the stove, but we prefer the extra timing buffer the oven's gentle, even heat offers.) The method works best with thin white flaky fillets. For a nice touch, fold fresh herbs—dill, tarragon, chives, parsley—and/or seeded, diced tomatoes into the sauce at the end.

4 tablespoons unsalted butter, cubed, plus extra for greasing the pan

1 large shallot, very thinly sliced

Leaves from 3 sprigs thyme or 1/2 scant teaspoon dried

1 1/2 pounds skinless thin white, flaky fish fillets, such as flounder, sole, or tilapia

Salt and pepper

1/2 cup dry white wine

1/2 cup low-sodium chicken broth

Fresh lemon juice

—Preheat the oven to 350°F, with a rack in the lower third position. Butter a flame-proof baking dish (not Pyrex) just large enough to hold the fish in a single, cozy layer (some overlap is okay), then sprinkle the dish with the shallots and thyme. Season the fillets with salt and pepper and put them in the dish skinned-side down. If you're using fillets with much thinner ends, tuck them under so they don't cook too fast.

—Add the wine and broth. The liquid should almost cover the fillets; adjust as needed. Put the dish over medium heat. As soon as the liquid starts to simmer, remove from the heat, cover the dish with foil, and poach in the oven until just cooked through, 4 to 7 minutes.

—Transfer the fillets to plates (if you can warm the plates first, that will keep the thin fillets hotter longer; you could also put them on a platter and tent with foil), leaving behind as many of the shallots as possible. Put the baking dish over high heat and boil the liquid until it's reduced to about 1/3 cup or is almost syrupy.

—Reduce the heat to low and whisk in the butter, 1 cube at a time. If the sauce starts to break, remove it from the heat for a few moments before proceeding; if it gets too thick, raise the heat a bit. Whisk in a small squeeze of lemon juice and check the seasonings. Spoon the sauce over the fillets and serve.

TIP: It may seem odd to poach fish in chicken broth. Fish stock is the classic choice, but we never have any and are guessing you don't either. Water is common, too, but it doesn't lend any flavor unless you take an extra 15 minutes or so and simmer some aromatics in it first. If you do opt for water, that's fine. Just avoid water that you wouldn't readily drink. Any funky, minerally tastes will show up in the poached fish and sauce.

BROILED FISH WITH TANGY TARRAGON MAYO

SERVES 4

We learned this clever technique for broiling fish from one of our favorite cookbooks: FISH by Rick Moonen and Roy Finamore. Preheating an ovenproof pan under the broiler helps cook the fish from the bottom up and gives it a nice sear. You can use this method for pretty much any type of fish (and on one large piece as well), but the tangy tarragon-flecked mayonnaise is particularly good on flounder, tilapia, cod, halibut, and salmon. Note that the thicker fish will take longer to cook.

—Preheat the broiler, with a rack positioned so that the fish will be 4 to 6 inches from the heat. Put a large cast-iron or other ovenproof pan on the rack and heat until very hot, about 5 minutes. Meanwhile, in a small bowl, stir together the mayonnaise, mustard, tarragon, and garlic, then season with salt and pepper.

—Lightly coat the fish with oil, season with salt and pepper, then cover the nonskinned side with the mayonnaise mixture. Carefully transfer the fish, mayonnaise-side up, to the hot pan. Broil until the fish is just cooked through and the mayonnaise has turned into a light brown crust, 3 to 8 minutes, depending on the thickness. Serve with the lemon wedges.

$1/4$ cup mayonnaise

2 teaspoons whole-grain mustard

Leaves from 2 sprigs tarragon, roughly chopped

1 garlic clove, minced

Salt and pepper

Four 6-ounce skinless flounder, tilapia, cod, halibut, or salmon fillets

Olive oil for coating

Lemon wedges

SAUTÉED TILAPIA WITH CITRUS-SOY MARINADE

SERVES 4

Shortly before our deadline, Caroline came home from a dinner at her friend Sujin's house raving about a soy- and orange-flavored fish dish. "She made it in, like, 2 seconds while we were all standing around and it was so good," she said. "Even the kids ate it all up." Of course, we had to get the recipe, and one test later it was in the book. (Full disclosure: We substituted honey for agave syrup, which isn't a staple pantry item for most people. But if you prefer agave, use it.)

In place of tilapia, Sujin uses other meaty fish, such as sea bass or salmon, that have been skinned. The cooking time will vary depending on the thickness.

$^2/_3$ cup orange juice

$^1/_3$ cup soy sauce

1 tablespoon honey

Four 6-ounce tilapia fillets

1 tablespoon vegetable oil, plus extra, if needed

—Put a gallon-size resealable plastic bag in a medium bowl to hold it steady. Add the orange juice, soy sauce, and honey, stirring until the honey is dissolved. Add the fillets and seal the bag, pressing out any excess air, and turn it over a few times to coat the fillets. Marinate at room temperature for 15 to 20 minutes (any longer and they might get mushy), turning the bag halfway through. Remove the fillets from the bag, reserving the marinade, and pat dry.

—In a large nonstick skillet, heat the oil over medium-high heat until it shimmers. Add the fillets, in batches if needed, and cook until golden brown, about 3 minutes. Flip the fillets over and cook until just cooked through, about 3 minutes more.

—Transfer the fillets to plates, add about half of the reserved marinade to the pan (discarding the remaining marinade), and boil until it coats the back of a spoon. Check the seasonings, then pour the sauce over the fillets and serve.

TIP: Here's an effortless method for getting every last sticky drop of honey (or maple syrup, etc.) out of measuring cups and spoons: Lightly coat them with some oil or cooking spray before measuring the honey. When you turn them over, it will just slip right out.

TIP: A nonstick pan produces the best results, but if you prefer to use a regular pan to cook the fish, increase the amount of oil to 2 tablespoons.

THE LINE ON SEAFOOD

Seafood can be one of the most satisfying and easiest things to prepare. That said, deciding what types to include in our book wasn't easy. Not only does the selection differ somewhat depending on where people live, the issues of safety and sustainability are complex and seem to get more confusing all the time.

To help make sense of it all, we rely on the Monterey Bay Aquarium Seafood Watch Guides (visit http://www.montereybayaquarium.org/cr/seafoodwatch.aspx to order a pocket guide, print a copy, or download a mobile version). These trusty and continually updated US-oriented resources are organized by region and classify the most commonly available seafood into one of three categories—Best Choices, Good Alternatives, and Avoid—and detail the way they are raised or caught, if relevant.

For instance, at the time of publication, US-farmed tilapia was listed under "Best Choices," tilapia farmed in Central and South America under "Good Alternatives," and Asia-farmed tilapia under "Avoid." So to make the smartest "ocean friendly" selections, be sure to educate yourself and ask where your seafood comes from and how it was raised and/or caught.

It's also very important to go shopping with an open mind, particularly since seafood is so perishable. If you're set on making salmon, but it looks like it's been kicking around for a while and the store just got in harpoon-caught swordfish, buy the swordfish, which is a fresher and more sustainable option. Our recipes are flexible and we've included possible substitutions in many cases.

GREEK-STYLE FISH WITH YOGURT AND LEMON

SERVES 4

This is a dish Caroline came up with when she couldn't resist buying some pristine halibut while vacationing in Maine. She was staying in a little rental cottage where the ingredients on hand were limited. But with good olive oil lugged from home, sprigs of dill pilfered from a neighbor's garden, some yogurt left over from breakfast, and one lemon, a Greek-style dish was born. Her inspiration? It's possible she had just watched Mamma Mia! *for the millionth time. . . .*

She now makes the dish regularly, using whatever large piece of thick white, flaky fish is freshest (individual 6-ounce skinless fillets can be used as well, although they will cook a little faster), and likes to serve it over orzo tossed with olive oil, salt, pepper, and sometimes a handful of feta. The flavors pair wonderfully and the pasta soaks up all the lemony juices.

—Preheat the oven to 450°F, with a rack in the middle position. Lightly coat the fish with oil, season with salt and pepper, and arrange skinned-side down on a sheet pan (lined with foil for easier cleanup, if you like). Top the fish with the lemon slices, drizzle with a little more oil, then roast until just cooked through, 10 to 12 minutes.

—Use a spatula to cut and serve the fish directly from the pan onto plates. Spoon any pan juices over top, then squeeze on the juice from the roasted lemon slices, taking care not to burn your hands and to remove any seeds. Top the fish with a sprinkle of salt, 1 or 2 spoonfuls of the yogurt, some dill, and drizzle with olive oil. You can also let people help themselves to the toppings at the table.

One 1½-pound piece skinless thick, white flaky fish, such as halibut, cod, or mahimahi

Olive oil

Salt and pepper

1 large lemon, thinly sliced

½ cup Greek yogurt

Handful of fresh dill, roughly chopped

FISH TACOS WITH PINEAPPLE SALSA

SERVES 4

Is it bad to say that the best fish taco we ever had was at an aquarium? During a visit to the aquarium in San Diego, Caroline and her family had lunch at the cafeteria, where they gleefully devoured the local specialty within feet of an ocean life display. Since then, Caroline has forced her family to sample many fish tacos in and around the San Diego area, but has yet to find better. That winning combination of crisp cabbage, creamy sauce, and tender, lightly spiced fish inspired this version, which we also like with Pineapple Salsa.

$^1/_2$ cup sour cream

Grated zest of $^1/_2$ lime, and juice

1 tablespoon water

1$^1/_2$ pounds skinless thick white, flaky fish fillets, such as halibut, cod, or mahimahi, cut into pieces about 4 inches long and patted dry

Salt and pepper

$^1/_2$ tablespoon ground cumin

1 teaspoon chili powder

2 tablespoons vegetable oil, plus extra, if needed

8 warm small flour tortillas (see Tip)

TOPPINGS OF YOUR CHOICE

Pineapple Salsa (recipe follows)

Large handful of cilantro, roughly chopped

Halved cherry tomatoes

Sliced avocado

Shredded green cabbage

Lime wedges

—In a small bowl, stir together the sour cream, lime zest, and water. Add a splash of lime juice, then set the sour cream sauce aside. Season the fish with salt and pepper, then sprinkle with the cumin and chili powder and rub to evenly distribute.

—In a large skillet, heat the oil over medium-high heat until it shimmers. Add the fish, in batches if needed, and cook until golden brown, about 3 minutes. Flip the fish over and cook until just cooked through, 3 to 5 minutes more. Transfer the fish to a platter. Serve with the warm tortillas, sour cream sauce, and toppings and let everyone assemble their tacos as they like.

TIP: If you have a favorite way to warm tortillas, use it. We usually wrap a stack of about 4 at a time in a layer of damp paper towels and microwave on medium-high for about 20 seconds or wrap the paper towel–covered stack in a layer of foil and bake in a 250°F oven for about 15 minutes. Either way, keep the tortillas wrapped until you're ready to use them so they stay warm and pliable.

PINEAPPLE SALSA MAKES ABOUT 1⅓ CUPS

This sweet, tropical salsa with a little kick really complements the fish tacos. It's also good with grilled meats and seafood. If you like a lot of heat, add more jalapeño.

—In a small bowl, stir together the pineapple, jalapeños, onions, and vinegar, then season with salt and pepper. Check the seasonings. The Pineapple Salsa will keep, covered in the refrigerator, for about 4 days.

1 cup finely diced pineapple (from about ¼ pineapple)

½ jalapeño, seeded and finely chopped

½ small red onion, finely chopped

2 tablespoons white wine vinegar

Salt and pepper

IS IT BAD TO SAY THAT THE BEST FISH TACO WE EVER HAD WAS AT AN AQUARIUM?

THE COMBINATION OF CRISP CABBAGE, CREAMY SAUCE, AND TENDER, LIGHTLY SPICED FISH . . . MMM

—*See Fish Tacos, page 32*

FISH FINGERS WITH LIME-GINGER DIPPING SAUCE

SERVES 4

Depending on where you grew up and your family's eating habits, the words "fish fingers" will likely evoke memories of a Friday night fish fry or your mom reaching deep into the freezer for a box of rock-hard batons. Our version actually borrows from both styles: These fish fingers are light, breadcrumb-based, and pan-fried (deep-frying fish is a sure way to make your kitchen smell like the Gorton's Fisherman's boat on a long August afternoon). They're also adult-approved. The Lime-Ginger Dipping Sauce is a tasty accompaniment, as is Tartar Sauce (page 38) or a simple squeeze of lemon or lime juice.

½ cup all-purpose flour

2 large egg whites

2 tablespoons soy sauce

2 cups panko breadcrumbs

1½ pounds thick white, flaky fish fillets, such as halibut, cod, or mahimahi, cut into 4 x 1-inch strips and patted dry

Salt and pepper

Vegetable oil for pan-frying

Lime-Ginger Dipping Sauce (optional; recipe follows)

——Put the flour on a large plate. In a shallow bowl, whisk together the egg whites and soy sauce until frothy. Put the panko in a deep dish.

——Season the fish with salt and pepper. Working with a few pieces at a time, dredge the fish strips in the flour, coating completely, then shake off any excess. Dip them in the egg mixture, letting any excess drip off, then coat them with the panko, gently pressing them into the breadcrumbs so they stick. Put the pieces on a platter large enough to fit all of them without crowding and repeat until all of the fish is breaded. If you have room in your refrigerator, chill the fish while the oil heats; it will help firm up the breading.

——In a large skillet, heat about ⅓ inch of oil over medium heat. Working in batches, add the fish and cook until golden brown and just cooked through, 2 to 3 minutes per side. Transfer the fish to a paper towel–lined platter and tent with foil to keep warm. Repeat with the remaining fish. Serve with the Lime-Ginger Dipping Sauce, if you like.

LIME-GINGER DIPPING SAUCE   MAKES ²/₃ CUP

You can serve this sweet, salty, citrusy, gingery sauce with a variety of foods, including cold soba or udon noodles; poached, roasted, or grilled vegetables, meat, or seafood; and the roasted shrimp on page 20. Omit the jalapeño if you don't want any heat. For a quick Asian-inspired chicken salad, toss the sauce with some store-bought rotisserie chicken, chopped scallions and cilantro or mint, and toasted sesame seeds. Wrap in butter lettuce leaves or spoon over steamed rice, if you like.

——In a small bowl, whisk together the sesame oil, soy sauce, vinegar, honey, lime juice, ginger, and jalapeño (if using). Check the seasonings. The Lime-Ginger Dipping Sauce will keep, covered in the refrigerator, for up to 3 days.

2 tablespoons sesame oil

2 tablespoons soy sauce

2 tablespoons rice vinegar (not seasoned)

1 tablespoon honey

Juice of 1 lime

1 tablespoon grated peeled fresh ginger

1 jalapeño, seeded and finely chopped (optional)

 TIP: Grating ginger is faster and easier than finely chopping it. Plus, the flavor of grated ginger infuses a dish more fully and evenly than that of chopped ginger (as such, if you're substituting the latter, you'll probably need to increase the amount by double or so). A zester will work; the smallest holes on a box grater are even better. Peeling is optional. If you regularly grate ginger, you may want to buy a traditional ceramic or metal ginger grater. Available at Asian grocers and some kitchenware shops, they're inexpensive and a breeze to use: The grated ginger collects in a little trough at the bottom of the grater and any tough, fibrous bits are left behind.

SALMON PITA BURGERS WITH TARTAR SAUCE

SERVES 4

"Burger" may not be an accurate description: We use salmon fillets because they eliminate the need to chop the fish, mix in any binders, and form patties, but they taste just as good. And we serve them in pitas because they hold the fish, toppings, and spicy juices together better than buns.

Grated zest of 1 lemon

$^1/_2$ teaspoon garlic powder

$^1/_2$ teaspoon ground cumin

$^1/_2$ teaspoon dried thyme

$^1/_8$ teaspoon chile powder

Four 6-ounce skinless salmon fillets, patted dry

Salt and pepper

1 tablespoon vegetable oil

2 pitas, halved and split open (we like the thick, whole wheat variety)

TOPPINGS OF YOUR CHOICE

Tartar Sauce (recipe follows)

Lettuce (Boston or red leaf are particularly nice)

Sliced tomato

Sliced red onion

Dill pickles

— In a small bowl, stir together the lemon zest, garlic powder, cumin, thyme, and chile powder. Season the fillets with salt and pepper, then coat with the spice mix, gently pressing it onto the fish.

— In a large skillet, heat the oil over medium heat until it shimmers. Add the fillets and cook until golden brown, about 4 minutes. Flip the fillets over and cook until almost cooked through, 2 to 4 minutes more. Put a fillet inside each pita half and serve with toppings. Let everyone assemble their "burgers" as they like.

$^1/_2$ cup mayonnaise

1 teaspoon whole-grain mustard

1 teaspoon prepared horseradish

2 tablespoons capers, chopped

Handful of flat-leaf parsley or fresh dill, chopped

Fresh lemon juice

Salt and pepper

TARTAR SAUCE MAKES $^3/_4$ CUP

Homemade tartar sauce takes only a few minutes to prepare and tastes so much fresher than the bottled variety. We like the simple briny bite of capers on its own, but feel free to add or substitute dill pickles or sweet pickle relish, if you like. If possible, make the sauce a few hours before serving so the flavors have time to meld. Serve it with the Salmon Pita Burgers, Fish Fingers (page 36), or as you would any tartar sauce.

— In a small bowl, stir together the mayonnaise, mustard, horseradish, capers, herbs, and a small squeeze of lemon juice. Season with salt and pepper, then check the seasonings. The Tartar Sauce will keep, covered in the refrigerator, for up to 2 days.

MISO-GLAZED SALMON

SERVES 4

There's something about slightly charred miso that is just so ridiculously good. Maybe that's why there are countless versions of this dish. It's like the molten chocolate cake of the fish world. Ours is based on one Kathy learned how to make when she lived in Japan (we substitute white wine and sugar for sake and mirin), and it's such an ideal weeknight keeper, we couldn't help but include it.

When broiled, the miso marinade caramelizes into a salty-sweet coating that pairs wonderfully with the rich salmon. The dish is easy to make, but it's best when the salmon has marinated for at least 8 hours, so plan accordingly.

—Put a gallon-size resealable plastic bag in a medium bowl to hold it steady. Add the miso, wine, and sugar and mash together until smooth by massaging the bag with your hands. Add the fillets, seal the bag, pressing out any excess air, and turn it over a few times to coat the fish. Marinate in the refrigerator for at least 8 hours, or up to 2 days.

—Preheat the oven to 400°F, with one rack in the middle position and another so that the fish will be 3 to 4 inches from the broiler. Line a sheet pan with foil for easier cleanup, if you like, then lightly grease with oil. Remove the fillets from the bag, letting any excess marinade drip off, and lay the fillets on the pan skin-side down.

—Roast on the middle rack until very rare (it will be very squishy when prodded with a finger), about 7 minutes. Remove from the oven and preheat the broiler. Flip the fillets over and broil on the upper rack until the miso starts to char in places and the fish is almost cooked through, about 2 minutes. (If you want to cook your fish a little more and the miso risks burning, cover the top of the fillets with foil.) Let rest for a couple minutes, then serve.

¹/₂ cup white miso paste

2 tablespoons dry white wine

3 tablespoons sugar

Four 6-ounce salmon fillets, about 1 inch thick

Vegetable oil for greasing the pan

TIP: Salmon is most luscious when it isn't cooked through, so we generally serve it still "pink" in the middle, or "almost" cooked through. If you've only ever eaten it medium or well-done, try it on the rarer side. If you don't like it, you can always cook it more.

SALMON IN FOIL WITH SPINACH AND CREAM

SERVES 4

When cooking "en papillote" (in a parchment paper packet), we usually use foil because it's always on hand and is easier to seal. Just take care not to poke a hole in it because you'll lose the juices, which help steam the food and keep it moist. The herbs are optional, but enhance both the spinach and salmon. Serve with rice, couscous, orzo, or crusty bread and dinner is done.

4 large handfuls of baby spinach

1 shallot, minced

2 tablespoons chopped fresh tarragon or dill, plus 2 tablespoons

Salt and pepper

Four 6-ounce skinless salmon fillets, about 1 inch thick

Grated zest of 1 lemon

1 cup heavy cream

——Preheat the oven to 425°F, with a rack in the middle position. In a large bowl, combine the spinach, shallots, and the 2 tablespoons herbs, then season with salt and pepper. Lay 4 pieces of foil, about 18 x 15 inches each, on the counter. Divide the spinach mixture among the pieces of foil, mounding it in the center in the general shape of the fillets.

——Season the salmon with salt and pepper, then put it on top of the spinach, skinned-side down. Sprinkle each piece of salmon with one-fourth of the lemon zest and 1½ teaspoons of the remaining herbs, then bring up the sides of the foil to create a bowl. Pour ¼ cup of the cream into the bottom of each packet. Leaving an air pocket over the salmon, fold together the edges of the foil along the top and both sides, tightly sealing.

——Put the packets on a sheet pan and bake until the salmon is almost cooked through, 9 to 12 minutes. (Test one fillet on the earlier side and add more cooking time if needed.) Transfer the packets to plates and serve. If you like, spoon whatever starch or grain you're serving into the opened packets so that it can absorb some of the sauce.

THE WHOLE PACKAGE

We love cooking en papillote because it's:

CONVENIENT. It's fast, easy, involves very little mess, and you can assemble the packets up to 2 hours ahead of time, then store them in the refrigerator, which makes them ideal for a dinner party.

VERSATILE. Once you learn the basic technique, experiment with combining different types of fish, adjusting the cooking time according to the thickness; liquids (wine, vermouth, olive oil, stock, soy sauce, sesame oil); flavorings (ginger, lemongrass, garlic, capers, herbs, spices); and vegetables (leeks, peas, snow peas, tomatoes, mushrooms). Just make sure you cut the vegetables small enough, or blanch them first, so they cook in the allotted time. And if you're using acidic ingredients, such as wine or tomatoes, switch to parchment paper because they may react with the foil, creating a funny taste and/or eating holes through it.

If using parchment, take a 15 x 24-inch piece, fold it in half crosswise, and cut it into a heart. Lay it out flat with the tip pointing at you. Put the ingredients for one portion on one half of the heart, then fold the other half over it. Starting from the bottom, fold about 1 inch of the edge of the parchment about ¼ inch toward the center, repeating as you work your way up to the top of the heart and slightly overlapping the folds. Press on the folds to help seal the package. Repeat with the remaining fish. If you would like a visual of this, search "folding parchment cooking" on the Internet; the methods may not match exactly, but will be close enough to help you along.

HEALTHFUL. Yes, the recipe on the opposite page uses cream, but in general very little fat, if any, is needed for super-flavorful results.

FUN. Everyone gets a "present" at the table; the bonus is the heady aroma that wafts out when the package is opened.

CLUCK!

CHICKEN AND TURKEY

MORNING CHICKEN

SERVES 4

We call this "morning" chicken not because it was meant to be consumed with your cornflakes, but because putting together a very quick marinade at the start of the day is all it takes to make a superior dish in the evening. While you go about your daily routine, the bird luxuriates in a mix of herbs and seasonings; 8 or so hours later, just pop it in the oven for about 30 minutes, then behold: crispy, mahogany-skinned pieces whose tender meat is imbued with garlic, mustard, thyme, lemon, and the warm smokiness of the paprika.

If you can't spare any time in the morning, marinate the chicken at room temperature for as long as you can (but no longer than an hour or so) before cooking. Any leftover meat makes a great lunch wrapped with some avocado and mayonnaise in a warm tortilla.

1 heaping tablespoon Dijon or whole-grain mustard

1 tablespoon smoked paprika

2 garlic cloves, smashed

Leaves from 4 sprigs thyme or 1 scant teaspoon dried

Grated zest and juice of 1 lemon

2 tablespoons olive oil

One $3^{1}/_{2}$- to 4-pound chicken, cut into 8 pieces, or $2^{1}/_{2}$ to 3 pounds chicken parts

Salt and pepper

—Put a gallon-size resealable plastic bag in a medium bowl to hold it steady. Add the mustard, paprika, garlic, thyme, lemon zest, lemon juice, and oil and stir to combine. Add the chicken, seal the bag, pressing out any excess air, and turn it over a few times to coat all the pieces. Marinate in the refrigerator for 8 to 12 hours (or at room temperature for up to 1 hour), turning the bag over once or twice, if possible.

—Preheat the oven to 450°F, with a rack in the middle position. Remove the chicken from the bag, letting any excess marinade drip off, and put on a sheet pan (lined with foil for easier cleanup, if you like). Season with salt and pepper and arrange skin-side down. Roast until golden brown, about 20 minutes. Flip the pieces over and roast until cooked through, about 10 minutes more. (If you're using wings, which cook faster, cook them until golden brown, about 20 minutes total, flipping halfway through.) Serve hot or at room temperature.

 TIP: We're picky about adding spices to our shelves, but will always make room for smoked Spanish paprika, or Pimentón de la Vera. Made from peppers dried over an oak wood fire, it's an essential ingredient in paella, chorizo, and many other traditional Spanish preparations, lending a beguiling smoky, woodsy flavor. In addition to this chicken dish, we add it to grilled or roasted vegetables (particularly good with cauliflower and potatoes), buttered corn on the cob, garlic bread, marinades or rubs for seafood and meat (see the fajitas on page 82), chickpea and lentil stews, tomato soup, tuna salad, deviled eggs, or practically anywhere you would use regular paprika.

For a quick dip, stir together some mayonnaise, smoked paprika, lemon or lime juice, salt, and maybe cayenne. And for the best fried eggs, cook them in olive oil and season before flipping with smoked paprika and salt, then serve topped with the flavored oil. Note that a little smoked paprika goes a long way, so despite the heady aroma, use some restraint. The best brands are arguably La Dalia and La Chinata; there are also three types: dulce (sweet), agridulce (bittersweet), and picante (hot). We generally stock dulce.

DEVILED PANKO-CRUSTED CHICKEN THIGHS

SERVES 4

*These crunchy, oven-baked boneless thighs take that classic kid staple—chicken fingers—
to a juicier, zingier level without the frying. And they're just as good the next day in a sandwich,
or served on a green salad. You can also use bone-in thighs; add on about 10 minutes.*

—Preheat the oven to 425°F, with a rack in the upper third position. Line a sheet pan with foil for easier cleanup, if you like, then put a large wire rack on top and grease with oil. (If you don't have a rack or just don't want to deal with cleaning it later, you can roast the thighs directly on the pan.)

—In a large bowl, whisk together the eggs, mustard, tarragon, ¾ teaspoon salt, cayenne, and garlic powder and season with pepper. Add the chicken, toss to coat, then set aside. In a deep dish, stir together the panko, cheese, and melted butter. Remove the thighs from the egg mixture one by one, letting any excess drip off, then coat with the panko, gently pressing it into the panko so it sticks. Put the breaded thigh on the rack top side up and repeat until all of the chicken is breaded.

—Roast until the chicken is cooked through and golden brown, about 25 minutes (flipping halfway through if using just a pan). Serve hot or at room temperature.

Vegetable oil for greasing the pan

2 large eggs

2 tablespoons Dijon mustard

1 scant teaspoon dried tarragon

Salt

¼ teaspoon cayenne pepper

¼ teaspoon garlic powder

Pepper

8 boneless, skinless chicken thighs (about 1½ pounds total)

1½ cups panko breadcrumbs

1 cup freshly grated Parmesan or pecorino cheese

4 tablespoons unsalted butter, melted

CHICKEN AND ROOT VEGETABLE DINNER IN A POT

SERVES 4 TO 6

This is one of our easiest and most forgiving chicken dishes. You can assemble it in the morning sans the salt, then season and bake it in the evening. And because it's covered for most of the cooking time, the meat stays tender and moist, even if left in the oven a little longer than called for. You can also substitute different vegetables and herbs. We like to serve the dish with coarse sea salt and Dijon in little ramekins so everyone can help themselves.

6 carrots, cut on the diagonal into ¹/₂-inch pieces

4 unpeeled Yukon Gold potatoes (about 1 pound), cut into ³/₄-inch pieces

4 celery stalks, cut on the diagonal into ¹/₂-inch pieces

2 leeks (white and pale green parts only), halved lengthwise, rinsed (see Tip below), and cut on the diagonal into ¹/₂-inch pieces

3 garlic cloves, smashed

¹/₄ cup olive oil

¹/₄ cup apple cider vinegar

1¹/₂ teaspoons dried thyme, plus 1 teaspoon

1 bay leaf

Salt and pepper

One 3¹/₂- to 4-pound chicken, cut into 8 pieces, or 2¹/₂ to 3 pounds chicken parts, patted dry

——Preheat the oven to 375°F, with a rack in the lower third position. In a Dutch oven that will fit the chicken in a single layer, combine the carrots, potatoes, celery, leeks, garlic, oil, vinegar, 1¹/₂ teaspoons thyme, and bay leaf. Season generously with salt and pepper and toss together.

——Add the chicken and toss again. Arrange the chicken on top of the vegetables skin-side up, then sprinkle with a little more salt and pepper and the remaining 1 teaspoon thyme. Cover the pot and bake for 35 minutes. Raise the heat to 450°F, uncover the pot, and continue cooking until the chicken is just cooked through and lightly browned and the vegetables are tender, about 15 minutes more. Discard the bay leaf, check the seasonings, and serve the chicken and vegetables with the juices drizzled on top.

TIP: If you've never eaten leeks, which resemble huge scallions, you are in for a treat. A backbone of French cuisine, this member of the onion family has a beguiling mild, slightly sweet flavor. The greens are generally used in stocks, while the white and pale green parts are commonly poached in one piece and gratinéed or served cold with a vinaigrette; sliced and added to soups, stews, and braises; or julienned and fried for garnishing dishes.

Because leeks are grown in sandy soil, they can require a little care when cleaning (although some leeks aren't gritty at all), but the steps are simple: Pull off any ragged, tough outer leaves. Trim the root end, then cut the leek crosswise about 2 inches above the white portion (you want to include the pale green parts, but not the dark green leaves; reserve those for stock, if you like). Starting about 2 inches up from the root end, slice the leek in half lengthwise. Rinse the leek root-end up under cold running water, gently pulling apart each layer of leaves so the water can run over and down them, taking any sand with it. (Holding it sideways or upside down may push any sand further into the leaves.) Shake the leek to remove any excess water, then pat dry or let air-dry upside down.

COCONUT CHICKEN CURRY

SERVES 6

A good, fast Indian yellow curry—redolent of warm spices and coconut milk—is a great dish to have in your weeknight arsenal. We love it as a simple meal served over steamed rice (basmati is traditional), but you can also easily dress it up by offering small bowlfuls of toppings, such as chopped toasted cashews, chopped cilantro, raisins, and/or lightly toasted coconut flakes. Toasting the coconut isn't essential, but Caroline had it that way once at the home of Indian friends and has never looked back.

—Season the chicken with salt. In a large skillet, heat the oil over medium-high heat until it shimmers. Add the chicken and cook until lightly browned, flipping the pieces over a few times, about 6 minutes total. Transfer the browned chicken to a medium bowl.

—Reduce the heat to medium, add the butter, and cook, swirling the pan until it's melted, until golden brown, about 1 minute. Add the onion, garlic, and ginger and cook, stirring often, until the onion is softened, about 6 minutes. Add the curry powder and cook, stirring constantly, until fragrant, about 30 seconds. Add the coconut milk and broth and stir to combine. Simmer, stirring occasionally, until the sauce thickens slightly, about 3 minutes.

—Add the browned chicken, along with any accumulated juices, and simmer, stirring occasionally, until cooked through, about 6 minutes. Add the spinach and stir until wilted, then season with lime juice. Check the seasonings and serve the curry with steamed rice.

1$1/2$ pounds boneless, skinless chicken thighs or breasts, cut into 1-inch pieces and patted dry

Salt

2 tablespoons vegetable oil

1 tablespoon unsalted butter

1 yellow onion, finely chopped

2 garlic cloves, minced

2 tablespoons minced peeled fresh ginger

2 tablespoons mild curry powder, such as Madras

One 13.5-ounce can unsweetened coconut milk

1 cup low-sodium chicken broth or water

4 large handfuls of baby spinach

Fresh lime juice

Steamed rice

CHICKEN MILANESE TOPPED WITH FENNEL SALAD

SERVES 4

This isn't a novel preparation, but it's a good one (even without the traditional pounding of the meat into thin pieces) and can stand alone as a meal. Mounding the salad on top of the chicken, with its crispy, featherweight crust, results in a wonderful combination of textures, temperatures, and flavors. The fennel adds crunch and an anise note, but if you don't care for it, leave it out and use extra lettuce—or top the chicken with your favorite salad instead. We also like to squeeze some extra lemon juice on the sautéed cutlets before adding the greens.

—In a large bowl, combine the oil, vinegar, and shallots. Season with lemon juice, salt, and pepper. Top—but don't toss—with the fennel, lettuce, and herbs, then set aside. (You will toss the salad just before serving.)

—Put the flour on a large plate. In a shallow bowl, whisk together the eggs and milk. Put the breadcrumbs in a deep dish.

—Season the cutlets with salt and pepper. Dredge one in the flour, coating completely, then shake off any excess. Dip it in the egg mixture, letting any excess drip off, then coat with the breadcrumbs, gently pressing it into breadcrumbs so they stick. Put the breaded cutlet on a plate large enough to fit all of them without crowding and repeat with the remaining cutlets.

—In a large skillet, heat ¼ inch oil over medium-high heat until it shimmers. Working in batches, if needed, add the cutlets and cook until golden brown, about 4 minutes. Flip the pieces over and cook until just cooked through, about 3 minutes. Transfer the cutlets to a paper towel–lined platter, sprinkle with salt, and tent with foil to keep warm. Repeat with the remaining cutlets.

—Transfer the cutlets to plates. Toss the salad with the dressing, check the seasonings, then mound on top of the cutlets and serve.

¼ cup olive oil, plus extra for pan-frying

2 tablespoons white wine vinegar

1 shallot, minced

Fresh lemon juice

Salt and pepper

1 fennel bulb, outer leaves removed, cored, and thinly sliced

4 large handfuls of lettuce, such as red leaf or butter, torn into bite-size pieces

Handful of fresh dill or flat-leaf parsley, chopped

½ cup all-purpose flour

2 large eggs

2 tablespoons milk

2 cups dried breadcrumbs

8 chicken cutlets (each about ⅓ inch thick, 1¼ pounds total), patted dry

TIP: You can easily make your own cutlets from chicken breast halves, which are generally less expensive, even if they're already boned and skinned. Put a boneless, skinless breast on a cutting board, lay your hand across the top, and gently press it against the board. Using a very sharp knife, cut the breast horizontally in half. Trim off any fat and flatten the pieces as needed with a meat mallet to an even thickness of about ⅓ inch.

MAPLE BARBECUE DRUMSTICKS

SERVES 4

Drumsticks are a fun choice, especially if you have kids, because they're easy to eat out of hand, but you can use other chicken parts, too. If you'd like to serve some of the Maple Barbecue Sauce on the side, make sure you portion that out before basting to avoid cross contamination with the raw meat. The barbecue sauce can be prepared right after the chicken goes in the oven.

8 chicken drumsticks (about 2 pounds total), patted dry

Salt and pepper

Maple Barbecue Sauce (recipe follows)

—Preheat the oven to 425°F, with one rack in the middle and another so that the chicken will be 3 to 4 inches from the broiler. Put the chicken on a sheet pan (lined with foil for easier cleanup, if you like). Season with salt and pepper and arrange top-side up and in alternating directions. Roast on the middle rack until golden brown, about 20 minutes.

—Brush some of the Maple Barbecue Sauce on the drumsticks, then flip them over and brush the other side. Roast until cooked through, about 10 minutes more. Remove from the oven and preheat the broiler. Flip the drumsticks over again, brush with more sauce, and broil on the upper rack until the sauce caramelizes, keeping a close eye on them to prevent burning, about 1 minute. Serve hot or at room temperature.

MAPLE BARBECUE SAUCE MAKES 1½ CUPS

While there's no shortage of bottled barbecue sauces, most contain preservatives and a fair amount of sugar. Making your own sauce is a snap and gives you the flexibility to control the acidity and heat. This version has a vinegary bite that's balanced by a touch of maple syrup, but feel free to play with the amounts to suit your taste. The sauce is also wonderful on shrimp and pork.

1 tablespoon olive oil

1 small yellow onion, finely chopped

1 garlic clove, minced

1 teaspoon salt

Pinch of cayenne pepper

$1/2$ teaspoon turmeric

$2/3$ cup ketchup

2 tablespoons maple syrup

$1/4$ cup apple cider vinegar

2 tablespoons whole-grain mustard

1 tablespoon Worcestershire sauce

Grated zest and juice of 1 lime

Pepper

—In a medium saucepan, heat the oil over medium-low heat. Add the onion, garlic, and salt and cook until the onion is softened, about 8 minutes. Add the cayenne and turmeric and cook, stirring, until fragrant, about 30 seconds. Add the ketchup, maple syrup, vinegar, mustard, Worcestershire sauce, and lime zest and stir to combine.

—Bring the sauce to a simmer, then season with lime juice, salt, and pepper. If the sauce needs more acid, add more vinegar or lime juice; if it needs more sweetness, add more maple syrup. If you're not using the sauce right away, let cool and transfer to a covered container. The Maple Barbecue Sauce will keep, covered in the refrigerator, for about 4 days. If serving as a dipping sauce, warm before using.

guitar
CONOR Soccer
Belle Soccer Game
ANNE of GREEN GABLES
By L.M. MONTGOMERY
DES MOTS POUR LIRE
à la maison
LAROUSSE
Vroom! Vroom!

MISO-LIME CHICKEN LETTUCE WRAPS

SERVES 4

Our families love this dish, which is sort of an Asian riff on Caesar salad. It includes anchovy paste, but it goes unnoticed by kids and adults. Dusting the chicken with Wondra flour before sautéing creates a delicate crust that helps absorb the miso-lime dressing. You can also use store-bought rotisserie chicken meat or plain grilled chicken. We sometimes make a salad instead of wraps with the ingredients: Chop the romaine and put it in a large bowl, shred the chicken and put it on top with the carrots and avocado, and toss everything with the miso-lime dressing.

1/4 cup honey

2 teaspoons white miso paste

1 tablespoon rice vinegar (not seasoned) or distilled white vinegar

2 garlic cloves, minced

1 teaspoon anchovy paste

1/4 cup vegetable oil, plus 2 tablespoons

Fresh lime juice

Salt and pepper

1/2 cup Wondra or all-purpose flour

8 boneless, skinless chicken thighs, or 4 boneless, skinless chicken breast halves, halved crosswise (about 1 1/2 pounds total), patted dry

8 large romaine lettuce leaves

2 large carrots, shredded

Sliced avocado

—In a small bowl, whisk together the honey, miso, vinegar, garlic, and anchovy paste. Slowly whisk in the 1/4 cup oil. Season with lime juice, salt, and pepper, then set the miso-lime dressing aside.

—Put the flour on a large plate. Season the chicken with salt and pepper. Dredge one piece in the flour, shaking off any excess. Put the floured chicken on a plate large enough to fit all of them without crowding and repeat with the remaining pieces.

—In a large skillet, heat the remaining 2 tablespoons oil over medium-high heat until it shimmers. Working in batches, if needed, add the chicken and cook until golden brown, about 4 minutes. Flip the pieces over and cook until just cooked through, about 3 minutes. Transfer the chicken to a paper towel–lined platter and tent with foil to keep warm. Repeat with the remaining pieces.

—You can let everyone assemble their own wraps: Put a piece of cooked chicken in the middle of a romaine leaf, top with some carrots and avocado, then drizzle with miso-lime dressing.

ADOBO-STYLE CHICKEN WINGS

SERVES 4

If you're not familiar with adobo—a vinegar and garlic–based dish and cooking method indigenous to the Philippines—we have three words for you: Try. This. Recipe. At one of the restaurants Kathy worked at in Hong Kong, the Filipino employees—a group of young women who loved to cook, eat, and laugh—regularly made it for staff lunch. It was a multinational kitchen and everyone had a say in what to serve, but these richly flavored tangy-garlicky adobo wings were always at the top of the list. Big bowls of steamed white rice and some kind of green vegetable stir-fried with garlic and ginger always rounded out the meal.

— In a large high-sided sauté pan with a lid that can hold the wings in a snug single layer, combine the water, vinegar, soy sauce, garlic, bay leaves, and peppercorns. Bring to a boil over high heat and boil for about 2 minutes. Add the wings, reduce the heat, and gently simmer, covered, until the wings are almost cooked through, about 15 minutes, flipping the wings over once.

— Meanwhile, preheat the broiler, with a rack positioned so the wings will be 3 to 4 inches from the heat. After simmering the wings, transfer them to a sheet pan (lined with foil for easier cleanup, if you like) skin-side down, leaving the liquid and any solids in the pot. Skim any fat from the surface, then boil the liquid until it's reduced to about 1 cup, about 10 minutes. Strain the sauce, if you like.

— Meanwhile, broil the wings until golden, about 5 minutes. Flip the wings over and broil until crisp and cooked through, about 5 minutes more. Serve the wings with the sauce on the side or drizzled over top.

1 cup water

³/₄ cup distilled white vinegar

³/₄ cup soy sauce

8 garlic cloves, smashed

3 bay leaves

1 teaspoon black peppercorns, lightly crushed

3 pounds chicken wings (about 16), halved at the joint and tips removed (save them for stock or soup, if you like)

TIP: There are probably as many variations of adobo as there are cooks who make it—and each, of course, thinks his or hers is the best. Some use more soy sauce than vinegar, others leave out the soy entirely; some use coconut milk in addition to or in place of the water, others don't use either; some add fiery chiles, others add ginger or sugar or all three. Then there's the whole issue of what protein (chicken, pork, seafood) and cut to use. Our advice is, once you get a feel for the dish, play with the ingredients to come up with the adobo that most suits your taste.

SAUTÉED CHICKEN WITH THREE PAN-SAUCE OPTIONS: GARLIC-CREAM, LEMON-ROSEMARY, AND TOMATO FONDUE

SERVES 4 TO 6

Sautéed chicken is great on its own (and at any temperature), but if you make it as much as we do, having a few pan sauces in your repertoire keeps things interesting and can elevate the dish, while adding only a few ingredients and minutes to the process. Boneless, skinless chicken is fine to use—and will cook faster—but bones and skin contribute lots of flavor. Lowering the heat and covering the pan after browning the chicken helps keep the meat moist and prevents the tasty bits on the bottom of the pan, which form the base for the sauce, from burning.

—In a large skillet or high-sided sauté pan with a lid, heat the oil and butter over medium-high heat until the foam from the butter begins to subside. Season the chicken with salt and pepper, then put in the pan skin-side down. Cook—resisting the urge to repeatedly poke, prod, and look underneath—until it doesn't stick to the pan and is golden brown, about 6 minutes.

—Flip the chicken over, reduce the heat to medium, and cover the pan. Cook until just cooked through, 10 to 15 minutes more. (If you're using both dark and white meat, note that the white meat will cook faster.) Transfer to a platter. If you're making one of the pan sauces, tent the chicken with foil to keep warm and continue with that recipe. If not, sprinkle the chicken with a little salt, and serve hot, warm, or cold.

1 tablespoon olive oil

1 tablespoon unsalted butter

One 3$\frac{1}{2}$- to 4-pound chicken, cut into 8 pieces, or 2$\frac{1}{2}$ to 3 pounds chicken parts, patted dry

Salt and pepper

GARLIC-CREAM PAN SAUCE MAKES ABOUT 1$\frac{1}{4}$ CUPS

—Pour off all but about 1 tablespoon of the fat from the pan of sautéed chicken, then return the pan to medium heat. Add the garlic and cook, stirring often, until fragrant, about 1 minute. Add the thyme and stir briefly. Add the wine, scraping up any caramelized bits from the bottom of the pan, and simmer until most of the wine has evaporated.

—Add the cream and any chicken juices accumulated on the platter and simmer until the sauce has reduced slightly and the flavor has concentrated, about 3 minutes. Check the seasonings, adding salt and/or pepper, if needed. Serve the chicken topped with the sauce.

4 garlic cloves, smashed

1$\frac{1}{2}$ teaspoons fresh thyme leaves or $\frac{1}{2}$ scant teaspoon dried

$\frac{1}{4}$ cup dry white wine

1 cup heavy cream

Salt and pepper

LEMON-ROSEMARY PAN SAUCE MAKES ABOUT 1¼ CUPS

1 garlic clove, minced

1½ teaspoons chopped fresh rosemary or ½ scant teaspoon dried

Pinch of crushed red pepper flakes (optional)

¼ cup dry white wine

1 cup low-sodium chicken broth

2 tablespoons fresh lemon juice

2 tablespoons unsalted butter

Salt and pepper

—Pour off all but about 1 tablespoon of the fat from the pan of sautéed chicken, then return the pan to medium heat. Add the garlic and cook, stirring often, until fragrant, about 30 seconds. Add the rosemary and pepper flakes (if using) and stir briefly. Add the wine, scraping up any caramelized bits from the bottom of the pan, and simmer until most of the wine has evaporated.

—Add the broth and any chicken juices accumulated on the platter and simmer until the sauce has reduced slightly and the flavor has concentrated, about 3 minutes. Off the heat, add the lemon juice, then swirl in the butter. Check the seasonings, adding salt and/or pepper, if needed. Serve the chicken topped with the sauce.

TOMATO FONDUE PAN SAUCE MAKES ABOUT 1½ CUPS

2 large shallots, thinly sliced

¼ cup dry white wine

1½ cups seeded and diced tomatoes or 1 pint cherry tomatoes, halved

1½ teaspoons chopped fresh tarragon, dill, chives, or a few torn leaves of basil

3 tablespoons unsalted butter

Salt and pepper

—Pour off all but about 1 tablespoon of the fat from the pan of sautéed chicken, then return the pan to medium heat. Add the shallots and cook, stirring often, until fragrant, about 1 minute. Add the wine, scraping up any caramelized bits from the bottom of the pan, and simmer until most of the wine has evaporated.

—Add the tomatoes and any chicken juices accumulated on the platter and cook, stirring often, until they are slightly broken down and heated through, about 2 minutes. If using cherry tomatoes, gently press them with the back of a spoon. Off the heat, add the herbs, then swirl in the butter. Check the seasonings, adding salt and/or pepper, if needed. Serve the chicken topped with the sauce.

TIP: It's an extra step, but skinning the tomatoes before seeding and dicing them yields a more delicate, refined sauce. To do so, cut a shallow cross at the bottom of the tomatoes, dip them in a pot of boiling water for 5 to 10 seconds, shock in a bowl of ice water, then peel off the skin. When you can't find good regular tomatoes, cherry tomatoes are the way to go. These we never peel.

CHICKEN AND RICE WITH GINGER-SCALLION SAUCE

SERVES 4 TO 6

Hainanese chicken rice—a popular dish of poached chicken and rice, usually served with the poaching broth and various sauces—originated on the island of Hainan, off China's south coast, and is now found in Malaysia, Singapore, and other parts of Southeast Asia. This pared-down version makes up in convenience for what it lacks in authenticity. If you're short on time, make the rice with low-sodium chicken broth instead of the poaching broth while the chicken cooks or serve plain steamed rice. But no matter what, don't skip the Ginger-Scallion Sauce. It is freakishly good and makes the chicken, as well as pretty much anything else, taste even better.

4 cups low-sodium chicken broth

4 cups water

Four ¼-inch slices fresh ginger, smashed

4 scallions (dark green parts only)

1 teaspoon salt, plus 1 tablespoon

4 bone-in, skin-on chicken breast halves (about 3 pounds total)

2 tablespoons vegetable oil

2 shallots, thinly sliced

1 large garlic clove, minced

2 cups long-grain rice, such as jasmine or basmati, rinsed

Sesame oil

Soy sauce

Ginger-Scallion Sauce (recipe follows)

Cilantro sprigs (optional)

Sliced cucumber (optional)

—In a pot just large enough to hold the chicken snugly, combine the broth, water, ginger, scallions, and 1 teaspoon salt and bring to a boil over high heat. Vigorously rub the chicken all over with the remaining 1 tablespoon salt. When the liquid comes to a boil, add the chicken skin-side down and weight down with an inverted plate. The liquid should just cover the chicken; if it doesn't, add enough water until it does. Reduce the heat and simmer gently for 12 minutes, then remove the pot from the heat and let the chicken rest in the hot broth until just cooked through, about 15 minutes.

—Meanwhile, fill a large bowl halfway with ice water. Reserving the poaching broth, transfer the cooked chicken to the bowl of ice water, let sit until cool for about 5 minutes to help set the texture, then drain and pat dry. (The chicken is traditionally served cool or at room temperature, but you can skip these steps, if you like.)

—While the chicken is cooling, start the rice. In a medium saucepan, heat the oil over medium heat. Add the shallots and cook, stirring often, until softened and lightly browned, about 4 minutes. Add the garlic and cook, stirring often, until golden, about 1 minute. Add the rice and cook, stirring often, for 1 minute. Add 3 cups of the reserved poaching broth and bring to a boil. Cover, reduce the heat to low, and cook until tender and the liquid is absorbed, about 20 minutes. Off the heat, let stand for about 5 minutes, then fluff with a fork.

—Remove and discard the chicken bones and the skin, if you like, and cut the meat crosswise into ½-inch pieces. Divide among plates, drizzle with some sesame oil and soy sauce, and serve with a big scoop of rice, the Ginger-Scallion Sauce, cilantro, and sliced cucumber, if you like.

GINGER-SCALLION SAUCE MAKES ABOUT ¾ CUP

Kathy has been addicted to this piquant, versatile green sauce (think Asian pesto) ever since her first taste at a Singapore hawker stall more than 20 years ago. Who knew the bracing combination of scallions, ginger, salt, and a little oil could be so good? We almost always double the recipe. Once it's in your fridge, you'll keep finding excuses to use it: a dab on steak, fish, or shrimp; mixed into noodles; as a topping on plain rice or with dumplings.

You can whiz the roughly chopped ingredients in the food processor—and we sometimes do—but that tends to break down the scallions, giving the sauce a duller color and a slight sliminess. The hand-chopped version requires a little more work, but yields a brighter, more textured sauce. (FYI, Caroline likes to add a splash of soy sauce to the Ginger-Scallion Sauce; Kathy doesn't. Try it both ways to see which you prefer.)

—In a small bowl, stir together the scallions, ginger, salt, and oil. Let sit for about 20 minutes, then check the seasonings. It should almost be "salty." The Ginger-Scallion Sauce will keep, covered in the refrigerator, for about 3 days.

1 bunch of scallions, very thinly sliced (about ⅔ cup)

¼ cup peeled finely minced fresh ginger

½ teaspoon salt

⅓ cup grapeseed, peanut, or vegetable oil

TIP: Hainanese chicken rice is often served with a chile sauce as well. Rather than make our own, we usually opt for Sriracha sauce, either alone or mixed with some lime juice.

TIP: Strain and use the leftover poaching broth as tradition dictates—as a simple soup to serve with the chicken—or save it for another use. It'd be really good in the Shrimp Wonton Soup (page 136) or with the Everday Pork Meatballs (page 95), for example. The broth will keep, covered in the freezer, for up to 6 months.

ROASTED CHICKEN BREASTS WITH SWEET POTATOES

SERVES 4 TO 6

One of the best dishes Caroline's ever had was at an outdoor food market in Paris. A vendor was selling rotisserie chickens that were spinning on rows of spits behind a counter. The birds were delicious, but the real treasure was at the bottom of the apparatus: a pile of small potatoes slowly cooking in the fat that was dripping on them. With the chicken, she was given a paper bag full of the hot and crispy potatoes, which she devoured right on the spot. Take note, American supermarkets!

Naturally, she had to re-create the dish after returning home; lacking a rotisserie, she set the bird in the oven right on top of the spuds. They don't get as crispy, but still soak up all the flavorful juices. On weeknights, she usually roasts chicken breasts because they cook faster than a whole bird. You can use unpeeled red or Yukon Gold potatoes, but after trying the method once with sweet potatoes, which get even more delectable, she's made the dish that way ever since.

4 sweet potatoes (about 2½ pounds total), peeled and cut into 1-inch pieces

2 tablespoons olive oil, plus 1 tablespoon

Salt and pepper

1 tablespoon finely chopped fresh rosemary

Grated zest and juice of 1 large lemon

4 chicken breast halves (about 3 pounds total), patted dry

¼ cup dry white wine

—Preheat the oven to 450°F, with a rack in the middle position. Put the sweet potatoes in a large roasting pan, sprinkle on the 2 tablespoons oil, season with salt and pepper, and toss until well combined. Spread the potatoes out in a single layer and set aside.

—In a small bowl, stir together the remaining 1 tablespoon oil, the rosemary, lemon zest, and lemon juice, and season with salt. Gently loosen the skin from the chicken breasts from the wider end and rub the mixture between the skin and the meat. Season the chicken with a little more salt and pepper, then put skin-side up in the pan on top of the potatoes and roast for 20 minutes.

—Gently toss the potatoes, sliding the ones under the chicken out and vice versa. Pour the wine over the chicken and continue to roast until the chicken is just cooked through, about 15 minutes more.

—Transfer the chicken to a cutting board, tent with foil to keep warm, and let rest for 5 to 10 minutes. If the potatoes aren't tender yet, return them to the oven. When they are soft, toss them again, scraping up any caramelized bits on the bottom of the pan. If you like, remove the meat from the bones and cut crosswise into ½-inch pieces. Serve the chicken with the potatoes.

CHICKEN POT PIE

SERVES 4 TO 6

Chicken pot pie is one of those foods that always makes us feel better. The combination of bright vegetables and tender chicken enveloped in a creamy sauce and topped with a golden crust is the very definition of comfort food. Fortunately, it's possible to make even on busy nights when you use store-bought puff pastry dough and bake the pie in a dish about the same size so there's no need to roll out or cut the dough. We usually use a 7 x 11-inch 2-quart rectangular baking dish with a sheet of Pepperidge Farm puff pastry, but you can fit the dough as needed based on the size of your dish and brand of pastry.

—Preheat the oven to 425°F, with a rack in the middle position.

—In a large skillet, add the oil and bacon and turn the heat to medium. Cook the bacon, stirring occasionally, until almost crisp, about 6 minutes. Add the garlic and continue to cook, stirring often, for 1 minute more.

—Raise the heat to medium-high, add the chicken, season with salt and pepper, sprinkle with the flour, and cook, stirring often, until the chicken is browned all over, 4 to 6 minutes. Stir in the thyme, broth, and Marsala, scraping the bottom of the pan to incorporate all the caramelized bits and flour. Bring to a boil, then reduce the heat and simmer until the sauce thickens, about 4 minutes. Stir in the vegetables. (There's no need to heat them through; they will cook in the oven.) Check the seasonings and transfer the chicken mixture to a 7 x 11-inch 2-quart baking dish.

—In a small bowl, whisk together the egg and water. Moisten the edges of the baking dish with water, which will help the puff pastry sheet stick to the dish so it doesn't shrink while baking. Carefully set the sheet over the dish. Working quickly so the heat from the filling doesn't soften it too much, pinch and crimp the sheet against the inside rim of the dish as in the photo opposite, gently stretching and/or folding it as needed; or, for a more rustic look, keep the dough draped over the edge and press any overhang against the outside of the dish. Pinch any holes closed and brush the pastry with some of the egg mixture.

—Put the pie on a sheet pan and bake until the pastry is puffy and golden brown, about 20 minutes. Let rest for about 5 minutes before serving.

 TIP: Marsala wine is a fortified Italian wine with a slightly sweet, smoky quality and is often used in cooking. It's worth picking up a bottle (a decent one will cost about $12) since it adds such a distinctive flavor, lasts for 3 to 4 months once opened, and is pretty versatile: You can use it to deglaze a pan after sautéing chicken or pork, or simmer it with sliced mushrooms and a pat of butter for a pasta sauce, or mix it with whipped cream to spoon over berries for a boozy dessert.

1 tablespoon olive oil

6 slices bacon, cut crosswise into ¹/₂-inch pieces

1 garlic clove, minced

1¹/₂ pounds boneless, skinless chicken thighs, cut into bite-size pieces and patted dry

Salt and pepper

¹/₃ cup all-purpose flour

2 teaspoons dried thyme

2 cups low-sodium chicken broth

3 tablespoons Marsala wine

One 16-ounce package frozen mixed vegetables, thawed

1 large egg

1 tablespoon water

1 sheet frozen puff pastry (see note above), thawed

SMOKY TURKEY CHILI

SERVES 8 TO 10

We're of the mind that if you're going to make chili, make a big pot. It'll keep in the refrigerator for about 5 days, so you can also eat it later in the week. Or freeze some and pull it out on one of those days when the idea of cooking dinner is as unappealing as a trip to the DMV. But if you want to make a smaller batch, just halve the recipe.

Chipotle chiles (also known as smoked jalapeños) in adobo sauce—a mixture of tomatoes, vinegar, spices, and garlic—are generally found in the Mexican section of the supermarket. They lend a unique bite of heat and a mellow smokiness. One can is more than you'll need here, so store the extra in an airtight container in the refrigerator, where it should last for months.

2 tablespoons olive oil, plus extra, if needed

2 pounds ground turkey, dark meat or a combination of dark and white

Salt and pepper

1 large white onion, chopped

3 carrots, chopped

2 celery stalks, chopped

1 heaping tablespoon tomato paste

2 chipotle chiles in adobo sauce (remove the seeds for a milder effect), minced

1 teaspoon ground cumin

1 cup water

One 28-ounce can crushed tomatoes

Two 15.5-ounce cans red, white, or black beans, drained and rinsed (see Tip)

—In a large pot, heat the oil over high heat until it shimmers. Add the turkey, season with salt and pepper, and cook, stirring often and breaking up the meat, until browned, about 6 minutes. Transfer the meat to a medium bowl and set aside.

—Reduce the heat to medium, add a little extra oil, if needed, then add the onions, carrots, and celery, season with salt and pepper, and cook, stirring occasionally, until softened, about 10 minutes. Add the tomato paste and stir for about 30 seconds, then add the chipotles and cumin and stir for about 30 seconds more.

— Add the cooked turkey and any juices, water, tomatoes, and beans and bring to a boil over high heat. (We generally prefer to use whole peeled canned tomatoes and crush them ourselves, but we like the ease and texture of precrushed ones here. Depending on the brand, the mixture may be a bit thick; if so, add another cup or so of water.) Reduce the heat and simmer, stirring occasionally, until the vegetables are tender and the sauce has thickened, about 30 minutes. Check the seasonings and serve the chili in bowls with toppings.

TOPPINGS OF YOUR CHOICE

Shredded sharp cheddar cheese

Diced avocado

Hot sauce

Sour cream

Sliced scallions

TIP: Our Everyday Black Beans (page 188) can be used in place of the canned beans and will make the chili even more flavorful. Substitute about 3½ cups cooked black beans.

TURKEY TACO NIGHT

SERVES 4

We've yet to come across a family that can resist the communal appeal of taco night, with everyone gathered around a table crowded with spiced meat and all the fixings. When we were kids, taco night was centered around a certain yellow boxed kit. Although we may have a little nostalgia for ground beef flavored with a mystery seasoning packet, we now prefer turkey flavored with our own combination of spices. It's almost as fast to make and is so much better tasting and more healthful. But, of course, we still let everyone assemble their own tacos.

—In a large skillet, heat the oil over medium heat. Add the onion and garlic and cook, stirring occasionally, until the onion is softened, about 6 minutes. Add the tomato paste and stir for about 30 seconds. Raise the heat to medium-high and add the turkey, oregano, cumin, chile powder, and cayenne pepper. Season with salt and pepper and cook, stirring often and breaking up the meat, until the turkey is browned and cooked through, 6 to 8 minutes.

—Add the water and briskly simmer, scraping up any caramelized bits from the bottom of the pan, until almost evaporated, about 1 minute. Add the vinegar and cook for another minute, then check the seasonings. Transfer the filling to a medium bowl and serve with the taco shells and toppings.

1 tablespoon vegetable oil

1 yellow onion, chopped

1 garlic clove, minced

1 tablespoon tomato paste

1 pound ground turkey, dark meat or a combination of dark and white

1 teaspoon dried oregano

1 teaspoon ground cumin

$1/4$ teaspoon chile powder

$1/4$ teaspoon cayenne pepper

Salt and pepper

$1/4$ cup water

1 tablespoon apple cider vinegar

8 taco shells

TOPPINGS OF YOUR CHOICE

Shredded sharp cheddar cheese

Shredded iceberg lettuce

Chopped tomato

Sliced avocado

Hot sauce

Sour cream

Lime wedges

"JUMP-IN-THE-MOUTH" TURKEY CUTLETS

SERVES 4

The Italian dish saltimbocca, which translates as "jumps in the mouth," is traditionally made with veal that is rolled up with sliced prosciutto and sage leaves. We tried it once with turkey when we had some cutlets in the freezer and were surprised by how good it was. Now we make it that way all the time, particularly since turkey is much more accessible and affordable than veal—and less controversial. We've replaced the rolling with wrapping the prosciutto around the cutlets because it's easier and avoids any question as to whether the inside is cooked through. Sometimes we dress up the cutlets by serving them on a bed of arugula with lemon wedges.

—Put the flour on a large plate. Top each turkey cutlet with a sage leaf or pinch of dried sage, then top with a slice of prosciutto and wrap it around the back of the cutlet, gently pressing to adhere (it's okay if it doesn't cover the entire back side).

—In a large skillet, heat 2 tablespoons of the oil over medium heat. Add 4 of the cutlets, sage-side down, and cook until golden brown, 2 to 3 minutes. Flip the cutlets over and cook until golden brown and just cooked through, 2 to 3 minutes more. Transfer to a platter and tent with foil to keep warm. Repeat with the remaining 2 tablespoons oil and 4 cutlets. (If the browned bits on the bottom of the pan start to get really dark, lower the heat. If they burn, the sauce will be bitter.)

—Pour off any excess oil, add the wine (if using), and briskly simmer, scraping up any caramelized bits from the bottom of the pan, until almost evaporated. Add the broth and briskly simmer, scraping the bottom of the pan if no wine was used, until reduced by about two-thirds, about 3 minutes. Stir in the butter and a little lemon juice. Check the seasonings, adding salt, if needed, and pepper. Pour the sauce over the cutlets and serve.

$1/3$ cup all-purpose flour

Eight 3-ounce turkey cutlets about $1/4$ inch thick, patted dry

8 fresh sage leaves or 8 small pinches of rubbed dried sage

8 very thin slices prosciutto (about $1/4$ pound)

2 tablespoons olive oil, plus 2 tablespoons

$1/4$ cup dry white wine (optional)

1 cup low-sodium chicken broth

3 tablespoons unsalted butter

Fresh lemon juice

Salt and pepper

1½ pounds ground turkey, dark meat or a combination of dark and white

¼ cup whole-milk Greek yogurt

Grated zest of 1 lemon

2 teaspoons Dijon mustard

Leaves from 4 sprigs thyme

Salt and pepper

Four ¼-inch-thick chunks sharp cheddar cheese, about 2 inches long and 1 inch wide

1 tablespoon vegetable oil

4 hamburger bun–style potato rolls, split

TOPPINGS OF YOUR CHOICE

Avocado Spread (recipe follows) or sliced avocado

Lettuce, such as Boston

Sliced tomatoes

Thinly sliced red onion

Pickles

1 avocado, pitted and peeled

2 heaping tablespoons sour cream

2 tablespoons white wine vinegar

Juice of ½ lime

½ teaspoon salt

Pepper

¼ cup grapeseed or vegetable oil

Small handful of cilantro, chopped

"JUCY LUCY" TURKEY BURGERS

SERVES 4

This burger—two patties surrounding a molten cheese core—was inspired by the specialty at Matt's Bar in Minneapolis, Minnesota, a local institution Caroline's in-laws introduced her to. Seduced after the first surprising bite, she borrowed the idea and used it at home with turkey burgers, adding yogurt for flavor and moistness. (A combination of equal parts lamb and beef works well, too.)

—In a large bowl, combine the turkey, yogurt, lemon zest, mustard, and thyme, then season with salt and pepper. Gently mix together with a fork or your hands.

—Divide the meat into 8 even-size balls. Gently press each one into a patty about ¼ inch thick. Put 1 chunk of cheese in the center of each of 4 patties, then cover with the remaining 4 patties. Seal the cheese inside by gently pressing the patties together all the way around the edges. Season the patties with salt and pepper.

—In a grill pan or large skillet, heat the oil over medium-high heat until it shimmers. Add the burgers and cook until browned on the first side, about 3 minutes. Flip them over and cook until browned and cooked through, about 3 minutes more. (If a bit of cheese oozes out, don't worry; the crusty bits left in the pan are the best part, so just peel them off and eat them.) Transfer the burgers to the buns and serve with toppings.

AVOCADO SPREAD   MAKES ABOUT 1 CUP

This creamy, tangy condiment is terrific on all kinds of burgers, as a replacement for the mayo on a BLT, as a dip for vegetables, even dolloped on scrambled eggs. You can also thin it out with a bit more oil to make a salad dressing. Thanks to the lime juice and vinegar, it won't readily discolor.

—In a food processor, combine the avocado, sour cream, vinegar, lime juice, salt, and a large pinch of pepper. Pulse a few times to break up the avocado, then gradually add the oil with the motor running and process until smooth. (It should have the consistency of mayonnaise.) Transfer to a bowl, then stir in the cilantro and check the seasonings. The Avocado Spread will keep, covered in the refrigerator, for up to 3 days.

MOOO! OINK!

BEEF AND PORK

LONDON BROIL TWO WAYS: WITH CHIMICHURRI SAUCE AND WITH MUSTARD BUTTER

SERVES 6

When we're craving a steak, but are counting our pennies or feeding a crowd, this is what we make. Just to clarify, though, London broil is technically a cooking method, not a cut of meat. The method essentially involves marinating a lean, tough (i.e., inexpensive) piece of beef; broiling, pan-frying, or grilling it to rare or medium-rare; then cutting it into long, thin slices. However, many stores sell beef labeled "London broil." It's generally top round, so just look for either name.

Broiling the meat is fast and involves the least fuss and mess, but we sometimes pan-fry or grill it. Either way, it's good on its own and even better slathered with the Chimichurri Sauce or Mustard Butter on page 76.

—Put a gallon-size resealable plastic bag in a medium bowl to hold it steady. Add the garlic, vinegar, oil, and beef. Seal the bag, pressing out any excess air, and turn it over a few times to coat the beef. Marinate at room temperature for at least 30 minutes and up to 1 hour, turning the bag over once or twice.

—Preheat the broiler, with a rack positioned so that the meat will be 3 to 4 inches from the heat. Line the bottom of a broiler pan with foil for easier cleanup, if you like, then top with the broiler rack. Remove the meat from the bag, allowing any excess marinade to drip off. Put on the broiler rack, discard any remaining garlic pieces, and season with salt and pepper. Broil the meat for 5 to 7 minutes per side for medium-rare. Transfer to a cutting board, sprinkle with salt, tent with foil, and let rest for 5 to 10 minutes.

—Cut the meat against the grain into thin slices. Top with any accumulated meat juices and serve with the Chimichurri Sauce or Mustard Butter.

5 garlic cloves, smashed

$^1/_4$ cup red wine vinegar

$^1/_4$ cup olive oil

2 pounds top round (or "London broil")

Salt and pepper

Chimichurri Sauce or Mustard Butter (recipes on page 76)

TIP: The cooking time will vary depending on how cold and thick the meat is and the power of your broiler. When in doubt, err on the side of caution; you can always broil it more if it's too rare. Keep in mind, though, that the meat will continue to cook a little as it rests and that inexpensive cuts like top round get dry and leathery when cooked to medium or beyond.

CHIMICHURRI SAUCE MAKES ABOUT 1 CUP

This piquant, vibrant green sauce is said to have originated in Argentina, but it is popular in many Latin and South American countries. We use it as a marinade for, or accompaniment to, grilled, broiled, or roasted meats, fish, or vegetables. It's also wonderful stirred into white or black beans, on crostini or boiled potatoes, and for sprucing up store-bought rotisserie chicken. There are lots of variations, but we're partial to this one. When we served it at a barbecue recently, one friend said it was so good she wanted to stick her head in the bowl and drink it.

2 garlic cloves, smashed

1 shallot, halved

Large handful of flat-leaf parsley

Large handful of cilantro

Small handful of mint leaves

Pinch of crushed red pepper flakes

3 tablespoons red wine vinegar

1 teaspoon honey

Salt

1/3 cup olive oil, plus extra, if needed

—In a blender or food processor, combine the garlic, shallots, parsley, cilantro, mint, pepper flakes, vinegar, honey, and a pinch of salt. With the motor running, add the oil in a thin, steady stream until it resembles a thin pesto. (If the sauce is too thick and you've added all the oil, add a little more.) Process until combined and a uniform green color, but be careful not to overdo it. You want the sauce to have some texture.

—Check the seasonings. If the sauce needs more acid, add a bit more vinegar and whir again; if it needs more sweetness, add a bit more honey. The Chimichurri Sauce will keep, covered in the refrigerator, for up to 3 days.

MUSTARD BUTTER MAKES ABOUT 1/2 CUP

Juicy steak topped with a silky mustard butter sauce is a French bistro classic we adore. This mustardy compound butter is much simpler to prepare, but still gets raves. The butter can be made well in advance and also pairs well with salmon, chicken, pork, lamb, green beans, or asparagus. (For more on compound butters, see page 162.)

4 tablespoons unsalted butter, softened

1 tablespoon Dijon mustard

1 tablespoon whole-grain mustard

Fresh lemon juice

1 shallot, minced

1/2 tablespoon chopped tarragon leaves (optional)

Salt

—In a small bowl, mash the butter with the two mustards and a splash of lemon juice until combined. Stir in the shallots, tarragon (if using), and a small pinch of salt. Check the seasonings. The Mustard Butter will keep, covered in the refrigerator, for up to 1 week or in the freezer for about 2 months.

BEEF STROGANOFF

SERVES 4

Don't be put off by recollections of school cafeteria versions—this is a stroganoff you will want to line up for. We use thinly sliced tenderloin and cook it briefly so it stays tender, and add just a touch of flour and a few spoonfuls of sour cream to create a delicate sauce with a slightly tangy richness. Serve the dish on a chilly night with buttered noodles, mashed potatoes, or wild rice and top with some chopped flat-leaf parsley or dill, if you like.

——In a large skillet, heat the oil over high heat until it shimmers. Season the beef with salt and pepper, add to the pan, and cook, stirring often, until almost cooked through, about 2 minutes. Transfer to a medium bowl and set aside.

——Reduce the heat to medium and add the butter. When it has melted and the foam has subsided, add the onions and cook, stirring often, until softened, about 5 minutes. Raise the heat to medium-high, add the mushrooms, season with salt and pepper, and cook, stirring often, until lightly browned, about 3 minutes.

——Add the flour and mustard powder and cook, stirring constantly, for about 1 minute. Slowly whisk in the broth, then simmer until the sauce is thickened and any raw flour taste is gone, 3 to 5 minutes. Add the reserved beef and any juices and stir just until heated through, about 1 minute. Off the heat, after the bubbles have subsided (see Tip below), stir in the sour cream. Check the seasonings and serve.

2 tablespoons vegetable oil

1 pound beef tenderloin, cut against the grain into very thin slices about 3 x 1 inch and patted dry

Salt and pepper

2 tablespoons unsalted butter

$\frac{1}{2}$ yellow onion, finely chopped

8 ounces button mushrooms, thinly sliced

2 tablespoons all-purpose flour

1 teaspoon mustard powder

$1\frac{1}{2}$ cups low-sodium beef broth

$\frac{1}{3}$ cup sour cream

 TIP: It's important to wait for the sauce to stop bubbling before stirring in the sour cream because sour cream may curdle if added to boiling liquids. Another method to avoid curdling is to "temper" the sour cream by stirring a splash of the hot sauce into it first to warm it, then adding the mixture to the pan.

SEASONING NOTES

A little salt, and maybe pepper, is often all that stands between mediocre-tasting dishes and really good ones. That's why all the recipes in our book include the reminder: "Check the seasonings." Sure, it might be that a dish also needs some lemon juice, or more thyme, etc., to come alive (see Taste, Taste, Taste in Cooking, page 16), but salt is usually the key. Knowing how to season food and when something is properly seasoned is instinctual for some (annoying) people, but fortunately it's also a skill that can be acquired.

One of Kathy's most vivid memories from cooking school is tasting a soup as it went from underseasoned to properly seasoned to overseasoned. Her instructor had all the students stand around the pot and sample a basic vegetable soup without any salt. "Blah," "Yuck," "It's just like water," they responded. Then he added a big pinch of salt and they tasted again. Same reactions. Over a few more rounds, though, things started improving. The flavor of the broth, the onions, the carrots, the herbs became increasingly pronounced, and then more harmonious. One more smaller pinch of salt, some additional stirring, and spoons went into mouths: "Oh my God," "Wow," "What a difference," people exclaimed. The instructor smiled, quieted everyone down, then pointed at the pot and said simply but effectively: "There's the soup."

He went on to gradually add more salt until the soup was inedible. By the end, the students were tired of tasting, but understood the importance of salt in a dish, what "properly seasoned" tasted like, and how to achieve it. You can do the same thing at home. Just don't be afraid to make mistakes when using salt—that's how you learn. Today's overseasoned soup is tomorrow's well-seasoned one. Here are some other tips to help ease the seasoning learning curve:

SEASON AS YOU COOK, NOT JUST AT THE END. It's the difference between building flavors and trying to shoehorn them into a dish. This is especially important when a dish involves different components that will be combined later (think ratatouille, lasagna, chicken and dumplings). Season each component separately.

IF YOU'RE GOING TO BE ADDING RELATIVELY SALTY ELEMENTS TO A DISH, such as chorizo, Parmesan, miso, bacon, or canned broth, keep that in mind as you season, particularly if you aren't familiar with the recipe or ingredients.

SIMILARLY, IF YOU'RE MAKING A SOUP OR STEW that has a long cooking time, go easy on the salt at the beginning because as the liquid reduces, the saltiness will intensify.

IF YOU PLAN TO MAKE A PAN SAUCE or reduce a braising liquid after cooking meat or fish in the same pan, only lightly season the protein before you cook it. Some of that seasoning will be left behind in the pan or pot when you remove it and might make the resulting sauce too salty and/or peppery.

LIGHTLY RESEASON MEATS AND FISH AFTER they are sautéed, basted, or grilled because some of the seasonings may have been left in the pan, washed off, or dripped off. We usually use the same salt we cooked with, but finishing salts, such as fleur de sel, which have distinct textures and flavors, are really nice, too.

USE A HEAVY HAND WHEN BOILING STARCHY FOODS like pasta and potatoes (the general rule of thumb is that the water should taste like the sea) and when seasoning them in general. They are like sponges when it comes to salt and soak it right up. Also use the "tastes like seawater" guideline when seasoning the water used to blanch or boil vegetables to flavor them and help keep their color bright.

SEASON A DISH A LITTLE MORE AGGRESSIVELY DURING COOKING if you're going to serve it cold. Chilling dulls the flavors in food, so a pea soup that's well-seasoned when hot will likely taste bland once it's cooled down. If you're worried about overseasoning, err on the side of caution; you can always add more salt or pepper after you've tasted the dish cold.

IF YOU DO HAPPEN TO OVERSEASON A DISH, there may be a way to salvage it. If it's liquid-based, such as a soup or stew, try adding pieces of peeled raw potato (which can easily be removed—and eaten—after cooking) or some raw rice (which can't, so make sure it'll work in the final dish). If it's a protein or vegetable, rinse it under water and then season again, if needed. Sauces can sometimes be fixed with a little cream or honey or vinegar, or by diluting with water or unseasoned stock.

PAPER-THIN BEEF WITH SNOW PEAS

SERVES 4 TO 6

If you're nervous about stir-frying because everything happens so quickly, don't be. As long as you have everything organized before you turn on the burner, you'll be fine. And the more you do it, the more comfortable you'll become. We've also simplified things here by combining the liquids so you can add them in one step.

In typical Chinese fashion, the beef is sliced really thin (okay, "paper-thin" is an exaggeration), briefly marinated, then flash-fried; the result is so tender it practically melts in your mouth. If you don't have a wok, try using a large high-sided sauté pan to catch any oil that may spatter when you cook the beef.

1 pound flank steak, cut against the grain into very thin slices about 3 inches long and patted dry

2 tablespoons cornstarch

1/2 cup low-sodium chicken broth

3 tablespoons soy sauce

2 tablespoons white wine

1 tablespoon sesame oil

1/3 cup vegetable oil, plus extra, if needed

1/2 pound snow peas

1 bunch scallions, cut on the diagonal into 3-inch pieces

1 tablespoon raw sesame seeds (optional)

Salt

Steamed rice

—In a medium bowl, toss together the beef and cornstarch, then let sit about 5 minutes. In a small bowl, combine the broth, soy sauce, wine, and sesame oil and set aside.

—Heat a wok or a large high-sided sauté pan over high heat until very hot, then add the vegetable oil. When the oil starts to smoke, add half of the beef and stir constantly with a spider or slotted spoon until it just begins to brown, about 10 seconds. The meat should still be pink in places. Transfer the meat to a strainer set over a bowl to drain any excess oil. Bring the oil in the pan back up to temperature, adding more if needed, and repeat with the remaining meat, adding it on top of the first batch in the strainer. Set the meat aside.

—Add the snow peas to the pan and stir constantly for about 1 minute, then add the scallions and stir constantly until wilted, about 1 minute. Add the sesame seeds (if using) and stir briefly. Add the broth mixture and bring to a simmer. Add the reserved meat and stir just until heated through, about 30 seconds. Be careful not to overcook or the meat will be tough. Off the heat, check the seasonings, adding salt if needed. Serve right away—the hotter the better—with steamed rice.

 TIP: Thinly sliced beef will be more tender than thick slices here. It's much easier to slice the beef really thin when it is partially frozen. If possible, pop it in the back of the freezer about 30 minutes before you plan to cut it; just remember to take it out before it freezes all the way.

BEEF FAJITAS WITH CHARRED TOMATO SALSA

SERVES 4

Like many people, we had fajitas for the first time as kids at a neighborhood Mexican place where a scorching-hot pan loaded with grilled meat, onions, and peppers arrived at the table with a flourish and a trail of smoke. Although our version doesn't provide the same sense of drama (and skips the peppers; we're not big fans, but you could certainly add them), it celebrates what people really like about the dish—succulent pieces of beef and a tangle of onions coated in spices and the act of assembling the fajitas themselves. Fajitas need little more than some good salsa and sliced avocado, but if you prefer other toppings, feel free to add them.

1 teaspoon ground cumin

1/2 teaspoon chili powder

1/2 teaspoon smoked paprika

Grated zest of 1 lime, plus half the juice

Salt and pepper

1 pound skirt steak

1 tablespoon vegetable oil, plus 2 tablespoons

1 large Vidalia or red onion, cut into thick rings

8 small flour tortillas (see Tip, page 32, for warming info)

Charred Tomato Salsa (recipe follows) or your favorite jarred salsa

Sliced avocado

—In a large bowl, stir together the cumin, chili powder, smoked paprika, lime zest, and lime juice, and season with salt and pepper. Add the steak and coat with the spice mixture.

—In a large skillet or grill pan, heat the 1 tablespoon oil over medium-high heat until it shimmers. Add the seasoned steak, reserving the spice mixture bowl, and cook until browned, about 4 minutes. Meanwhile, add the onions to the reserved bowl and toss with any remaining spices. Flip the steak over and cook until browned and medium-rare, about 3 minutes more. Transfer to a cutting board, reserving the pan, tent with foil to keep warm, and let rest while you cook the onions.

—Add the remaining 2 tablespoons oil to the pan and heat over medium-high until it shimmers. Add the onions and cook, stirring occasionally, for 3 minutes. Add a splash of water and continue to cook, stirring occasionally, until golden brown and just softened, about 3 minutes more. Check the seasonings, then transfer to a platter. Cut the steak against the grain into 1/4-inch-thick slices and arrange next to the onions. Serve with the warm tortillas, salsa, and avocado.

CHARRED TOMATO SALSA MAKES 1 CUP

Charring the tomatoes and jalapeño give this mild all-purpose salsa a smoky, rich flavor. It may sound strange, but it's also good as a gazpacho-like soup: Scale up the recipe, process the ingredients a little finer, and serve topped with diced avocado and fried tortilla strips, if you like.

——Heat a medium skillet or cast-iron pan over medium-high heat until very hot. Add the tomatoes and chile and cook, turning as needed, until blistered all over and a little blackened in spots. Transfer to a cutting board. Cut the jalapeño in half lengthwise, discard the seeds, and put in a food processor. Cut the tomatoes in half, discard the cores, and put in the food processor. (If you prefer, you can chop the jalapeño and tomatoes—and the garlic and cilantro—by hand instead and combine them with the rest of the ingredients in a bowl.)

——Add the garlic, cilantro, vinegar, honey, and lime juice and season with salt and pepper. Pulse until the ingredients are roughly combined, then add the oil and pulse until just incorporated. Check the seasonings. The Charred Tomato Salsa will keep, covered in the refrigerator, for up to 4 days.

2 tomatoes (about 1 pound)

1 jalapeño or serrano chile

2 garlic cloves, smashed

Handful of cilantro

1 tablespoon apple cider vinegar

1 tablespoon honey

Juice of $1/2$ lime

Salt and pepper

$1/4$ cup olive oil

JAPANESE-STYLE "MEAT AND POTATOES"

SERVES 4

This recipe is based on a popular Japanese stewed dish called nikujaga (niku *means "meat";* jaga *means "potato"), which Kathy's mom often made when she was growing up. It's home cooking at its best, the kind of food you want to eat when you're tired or in a funk or under the weather.*

Unlike in America, stewed dishes in Japan tend to be very light and contain only a small amount of liquid, which is more of a flavorful broth than a "sauce." Like most stews, though, it reheats wells and tastes even better when the flavors have had time to meld, so don't hesitate to make it in advance or to double the recipe to ensure leftovers. This is also a good dish for nights when people will be eating dinner at different times; just leave it on the back of the stove and spoon it out when needed. Serve with steamed rice, if you like.

2 tablespoons vegetable oil

³/₄ pound ground beef

1 yellow onion, halved lengthwise and thickly sliced

1 large carrot, halved lengthwise and cut on the diagonal into 1-inch chunks

1¹/₂ tablespoons minced peeled fresh ginger

¹/₄ cup dry white wine

1¹/₂ pounds potatoes (russets hold up well here), cut into 1-inch chunks

2 tablespoons packed light brown sugar

1 cup low-sodium chicken broth

¹/₂ cup water

¹/₄ cup soy sauce

Salt

2 scallions, thinly sliced on the diagonal (optional)

—In a medium saucepan, heat the oil over medium-high heat until it shimmers. Add the beef and cook, stirring often and breaking up the meat, just until it's no longer pink, about 2 minutes. Add the onions, carrots, and ginger and cook, stirring often, for about 2 minutes.

—Add the wine and briskly simmer, scraping up any caramelized bits from the bottom of the pan, until almost evaporated. Add the potatoes, brown sugar, broth, water, and soy sauce and stir to combine. (The liquid won't quite cover the solids.) Bring to a boil, then reduce the heat and simmer, partially covered and stirring occasionally, until the potatoes and carrots are tender, about 30 minutes. Check the seasonings, adding salt if needed. Serve hot or warm, sprinkled with scallions, if you like.

TIP: Ground beef that is 85 percent lean is preferable here. You can also use thinly sliced beef instead. Well-marbled cuts, such as rib eye, work best. Ground or thinly sliced pork is also an option.

OUR FAVORITE MEAT LOAF

SERVES 6 TO 8

There are countless meat loaf recipes in the world, but after trying this one, you may renounce all others: The meat is super moist and flavorful, the glaze is sweet and zingy, and because we shape the loaf wider and lower than is typical (think pillow, not football) and bake it on a sheet pan, there's more delectable browned crust for everyone to fight over. The meat loaf cooks faster that way, too. Thickly sliced leftovers paired with good crusty bread and a generous smear of mayo also make killer sandwiches.

Many supermarkets carry premixed packs of "meatball" or "meat loaf" meat, a combination of ground beef, pork, and veal. If yours doesn't, use one-third of each or half beef and half pork.

½ cup ketchup

½ tablespoon (or to taste) Sriracha or hot sauce of your choice

1 teaspoon apple cider vinegar

2 cups cubed bread (supermarket bakery bread is fine)

½ cup buttermilk or whole milk

1½ tablespoons olive oil

1 small yellow onion, finely chopped

2 small carrots, finely chopped

2 large garlic cloves, minced

1 teaspoon fresh thyme leaves or ½ scant teaspoon dried

2 pounds "meatball" or "meat loaf" meat (see note above)

4 ounces pancetta or bacon (about 4 slices), finely diced

1 large egg, lightly beaten

3 tablespoons Dijon mustard

2 tablespoons Worcestershire sauce

Salt and pepper

—Preheat the oven to 350°F, with a rack in the middle position. In a small bowl, stir together the ketchup, Sriracha, and vinegar, then set the glaze aside. In a large bowl, combine the bread and buttermilk and let soak while you prepare the onion mixture.

—Line a sheet pan with foil for easier cleanup, if you like, then set aside. In a large skillet, heat the oil over medium heat. Add the onions, carrots, garlic, and thyme and cook, stirring occasionally, until the onions and carrots are softened, about 8 minutes, then let the onion mixture cool for a few minutes.

—Gently squeeze the bread, discard the excess buttermilk, and return the bread to the bowl. Add the meat, pancetta, egg, mustard, Worcestershire, onion mixture, 1½ teaspoons salt, and ½ teaspoon pepper. Gently mix together with your hands until evenly combined.

—Turn the meat mixture out onto the prepared sheet pan and form a mounded loaf that's about 5 inches wide and 12 inches long. Coat the meatloaf with the glaze, then bake until cooked through (160°F on an instant-read thermometer inserted horizontally into the center), about 45 minutes. Let rest for about 5 minutes, then cut the meatloaf crosswise into slices and serve.

SICHUAN-STYLE PORK WITH TOFU

SERVES 4

Called mapo doufu in Chinese, this classic dish is said to have been created long ago in Sichuan province by a pockmarked (po) old woman (ma) who cooked for poor workers. A combination of ground pork and soft tofu in a ginger- and garlic-laced fiery bean-paste sauce that's typically served over steamed white rice, this is Chinese comfort food at its best. We've taken the heat down a few notches (and bypassed a couple hard-to-find ingredients, such as Sichuan peppercorns, fermented black beans, and Chinese rice wine), but if you like a lot of spice, add an extra spoonful of chili bean sauce. You can also use ground beef or turkey in place of the pork.

—In a small bowl, stir together the wine and 1 tablespoon cornstarch until smooth. Add the pork and gently mix together. Let marinate for about 5 minutes. In a small ramekin or tea cup, stir together the water and remaining 1 tablespoon cornstarch and set aside.

—Heat a wok or large skillet over high heat until very hot, then add the vegetable oil. When it starts to smoke, add the pork and stir constantly, breaking up the meat, just until it is no longer pink, about 30 seconds.

—Add the ginger and garlic and stir constantly until fragrant, about 15 seconds. Add the bean sauce and stir constantly until fragrant, about 15 seconds. Add the broth, soy sauce, and peas (if using) and bring to a simmer. Add the tofu, return to a simmer, and cook, stirring occasionally and gently to avoid breaking up the cubes, until hot, about 2 minutes. Check the seasonings, adding salt if needed.

—Stir the reserved cornstarch mixture again, then clear a spot along the side of the wok by pushing back the tofu and meat and stir in the mixture. Gently mix everything together in a folding motion and simmer until slightly thickened, about 1 minute. Serve hot, spooned over steamed rice, and top with a generous drizzle of sesame oil, some pepper, and a sprinkling of scallions.

2 tablespoons dry white wine

1 tablespoon cornstarch, plus 1 tablespoon

$^{1}/_{2}$ pound ground pork

2 tablespoons water

2 tablespoons vegetable oil

1-inch piece of peeled fresh ginger, finely chopped

2 garlic cloves, finely chopped

2 tablespoons chili bean sauce

$^{1}/_{2}$ cup low-sodium chicken broth

$2^{1}/_{2}$ tablespoons soy sauce

Small handful of frozen peas (optional)

One 14- to 17-ounce package of soft (not silken) tofu, drained, rinsed, and cut into $^{3}/_{4}$-inch cubes

Salt

Steamed rice

Sesame oil

Pepper

2 scallions, thinly sliced on the diagonal

TIP: You should be able to find chili bean sauce, sometimes called hot bean paste, in the "International" aisle of your supermarket. (A common brand is Lee Kum Kee.) It lasts practically forever in the fridge and can be used in dips, stir-fries, on meats and fish—wherever you want a rich, spicy note. In a pinch, you can substitute 2 tablespoons white or red miso paste and few shakes of crushed red pepper flakes or hot sauce for the heat.

WHEN TO ADD THE HOOCH

If you have children and are reluctant to use alcohol when you cook, keep in mind that when simmered for an hour or so, or boiled for a few minutes, most of it evaporates. Meanwhile, the flavor concentrates and highlights and complements the other ingredients, which is why alcohol, particularly wine, is so commonly used by chefs. But if you don't want your kids exposed to the taste of it at all, it's probably best to just leave it out. Unless it's an alcohol-based recipe, like coq au vin or a red-wine sauce, the dish will be fine without it. You can always add regular apple cider in place of hard cider (as in the recipe on the opposite page), nonalcoholic beer in place of regular beer (as in the mussels recipe on page 24), or a little lemon juice or vinegar if you omit wine and some acidity is needed.

If you do use wine, stick to dry lighter reds or whites. It doesn't need to be expensive wine (Haut Brion belongs in a glass, not a sauté pan), just an everyday wine that you would drink. Steer clear of "cooking wines," which usually contain salt and other additives. Since most of our recipes call for about ¼ cup, here's a way to avoid waste if you don't drink wine regularly: After you measure out the amount you need, pour the remaining wine into ice cube trays, freeze, then transfer the cubes to a freezer bag. (REMEMBER TO LABEL THE BAG: You think you'll remember what's in it and how old it is, but we never do.) Each cube is about 1 fluid ounce, so the next time you need ¼ cup of wine, just pull out 2 cubes. They should stay fresh tasting for 3 or 4 months.

PORK TENDERLOIN WITH DOUBLE-APPLE SAUCE

SERVES 4

Serve this throughout the fall and into the winter, when a variety of crisp, sweet apples are in season. We cut the fruit into wedges, combine them with sage, onions, and apple cider (hard or regular, depending on our mood and what's on hand), and cook them down with the tenderloin into a rich "double" apple sauce. Not only does the dish make a nourishing dinner on a brisk evening (a side of Soft Parmesan Polenta, page 186, Toasted Orzo Risotto-Style, page 189, or plain buttered noodles would be ideal), any leftover pork is great the next day in a sandwich with a slathering of mustard.

—Preheat the oven to 400°F, with a rack in the middle position. In a medium Dutch oven, heat the oil over medium-high heat. Season the pork with salt and pepper, add to the pot, and cook until golden brown all over, about 6 minutes total. Transfer the tenderloin to a plate and set aside.

—Add the butter to the pot and heat it over medium heat. When the foam subsides, add the onions, apples, and sage. Cook, stirring occasionally, until the onions and apples are softened and begin to caramelize, about 8 minutes. Add the cider and bring to a simmer, scraping up any caramelized bits from the bottom of the pot. Return the tenderloin and any accumulated juices to the pot, cover, and roast in the oven until almost cooked through, but still pink, about 10 minutes. (See page 91 for information on pork cooking guidelines.) Transfer the meat to a cutting board and let rest for 5 to 10 minutes.

—Meanwhile, briskly simmer the liquid in the pot, stirring occasionally, until slightly thickened, about 3 minutes. Check the seasonings. Cut the pork into ¼-inch-thick slices and serve topped with the onions and apple sauce.

1 tablespoon vegetable oil

1 pork tenderloin (about 1¼ pounds), patted dry

Salt and pepper

2 tablespoons unsalted butter

1 large yellow onion, halved lengthwise and thinly sliced

2 firm, sweet apples, such as Honeycrisp or Golden Delicious, peeled, cored, and sliced

4 fresh sage leaves, cut into slivers, or 1 heaping teaspoon rubbed dried sage

1 cup hard cider, such as Woodchuck Granny Smith, or regular apple cider

BRAISED PORK CHOPS WITH CITRUS GLAZE

SERVES 4

Topped with meltingly soft onions and a tangy-sweet glaze that Caroline claims is better than ice cream, these chops are hard to resist. The relatively fatty blade chop is the best type to use here, but rib chops are fine, too. Just avoid the leaner loin chops, as well as cooking the meat too fast, which will toughen it—or too long, which will dry it out. (Despite what we've been told over the years, pork doesn't need to be cooked to well-done in order to be "safe." It's fine to eat when still pink—145°F is now the official guideline.) No-Fuss Roasted Potatoes (page 192) or Roasted Acorn Squash with Jalapeño-Lime Butter (page 162) are good side dish choices.

—In a large high-sided sauté pan with a lid, heat the oil over medium-high heat until it shimmers. Season the pork chops with salt and pepper, add to the pan, and cook until golden brown, about 3 minutes. Flip the chops over and cook until golden brown, about 3 minutes more.

—Scatter the onions and garlic around the chops, then nestle the rosemary sprig into the onions (or, if using dried rosemary, sprinkle on top). Sprinkle the brown sugar over all, add the broth, and top each chop with 2 lemon slices. Reduce the heat, cover the pan, and simmer gently until the pork is almost cooked through, but still pink, about 10 minutes.

—Transfer the chops to plates or a platter, leaving the onions and lemons in the pan. Briskly simmer the liquid, scraping up any caramelized bits from the bottom of the pan, until syrupy, about 5 minutes. Off the heat, discard the rosemary sprig (if using) and stir in the butter. Check the seasonings. Serve the chops topped with the sauce, onions, and lemon slices. (Feel free to eat the slices, which break down and mellow during cooking.)

1 tablespoon olive oil

Four bone-in pork chops about ³/₄ inch thick, patted dry

Salt and pepper

1 large yellow onion, halved lengthwise and very thinly sliced

2 garlic cloves, smashed

1 sprig rosemary or 1 scant teaspoon dried

¹/₄ cup packed dark brown sugar

³/₄ cup low-sodium chicken broth

1 lemon, cut into 8 slices

2 tablespoons unsalted butter

ASIAN PORK SLIDERS WITH MAGIC MISO-MAYO

SERVES 4

As with Morning Chicken (page 44), this is a good example of how a few minutes at the start of your day can lead to an extra-tasty dish in the evening. Marinating the tenderloin in a pineapple juice and garlic mixture tenderizes it and imparts a savory-sweet flavor. If you can't spare any time in the morning, marinate the pork for as long as you can before cooking (up to an hour at room temperature; any longer and it should be refrigerated).

We coat the marinated meat with hoisin sauce, roast it, slice it, then put it on light, fluffy potato rolls with extra hoisin and sliced scallions. Some Magic Miso-Mayo and/or hot sauce are really good, too. You can also serve the pork and fixings in lettuce leaves or on bowls of steamed white or brown rice.

2 cups pineapple juice

2 garlic cloves, sliced

1 pork tenderloin (about 1¼ pounds)

1 tablespoon vegetable oil

Salt and pepper

⅓ cup hoisin sauce, plus extra for serving

8 dinner-size potato rolls, split

4 scallions (white and pale green parts only), thinly sliced on the diagonal

Magic Miso-Mayo (recipe on page 94)

Sriracha or hot sauce of your choice

— Put a gallon-size resealable plastic bag in a medium bowl to hold it steady. Add the pineapple juice, garlic, and pork. Seal the bag, pressing out any excess air, and turn it over a few times to coat the tenderloin. Marinate in the refrigerator for 8 to 12 hours (or at room temperature for up to 1 hour), turning the bag over once or twice, if possible.

— Preheat the oven to 400°F, with a rack in the middle position. In a medium ovenproof skillet, heat the oil over medium-high heat until it shimmers. Remove the tenderloin from the marinade, pat dry, then season with salt and pepper. Add the tenderloin to the pan and cook until golden brown all over, about 6 minutes total.

— Off the heat, brush the top half of the tenderloin with half the hoisin sauce. Put the pan in the oven and roast for 8 minutes. Turn the tenderloin over, brush the top half with the remaining hoisin sauce, and roast until almost cooked through, but still pink, about 6 minutes more. (See page 91 for information on pork cooking guidelines.) Transfer the tenderloin to a cutting board and let rest for 5 to 10 minutes.

— Cut the pork into ¼-inch-thick slices. Serve with the rolls, extra hoisin sauce, scallions, Magic Miso-Mayo, and Sriracha, and let everyone assemble their own sliders.

MAGIC MISO-MAYO MAKES ABOUT $\frac{1}{2}$ CUP

The inspiration for this lip-smacking condiment is a miso mayonnaise we discovered at a fancy pants food shop that quickly became habit forming. After tiring of schlepping to the store for our fix (and always leaving with a cartful of items we had no intention of buying), we created our own version, which we like even better. Store it in a squirt bottle (recycle a plastic mayonnaise or ketchup container) and put it on basically EVERYTHING: burgers, sandwiches, eggs, crudités, rice dishes, grilled steak or fish, directly into your mouth.... You can double or triple the recipe depending on how much you fall for it.

$\frac{1}{2}$ **cup mayonnaise**
1 teaspoon white miso paste
Fresh lime juice

—In a small bowl, stir together the mayonnaise, miso, and a squeeze of lime juice until smooth. Check the seasonings. The Magic Miso-Mayo will keep, covered in the refrigerator, for up to 2 weeks.

EVERYDAY PORK MEATBALLS

SERVES 4

We call these meatballs "everyday" because they are more versatile than the traditional Italian tomato sauce–coated variety. Lightly flavored with ginger, soy sauce, and sesame oil, they can be served with rice or other grains, slaws including the Asian-style one on page 182, over a bowl of udon noodles, or added to broths and soups. Kids—and adults—also seem to like them straight from the dish.

Here's another idea, borrowed from the wonderful Vietnamese sandwich banh mi: *Take a hero roll or a 6-inch piece of baguette and split it in half lengthwise, keeping the bread attached on one side. Spread Magic Miso-Mayo (opposite page) or plain mayonnaise on both halves, then add three meatballs, some shredded carrots, sliced cucumbers, cilantro sprigs, lime juice, and, if you like heat, Sriracha. Squeeze the halves together and enjoy.*

—Preheat the oven to 400°F, with a rack in the upper third position.

—In a medium bowl, beat the egg. Add the garlic, scallions, ginger, soy sauce, vinegar, sesame oil, lime zest, ¼ teaspoon salt, and ¼ teaspoon pepper and stir together. Add the pork and panko and gently mix together with a fork or your hands. (The mixture will be a little "wet" and soft.)

—Shape the meat mixture into about 16 Ping Pong-size balls and put in a baking dish (lined with foil for easier cleanup, if you like). Bake until just cooked through, about 15 minutes. Serve hot.

1 large egg

2 garlic cloves, minced

2 scallions (white and pale green parts only), thinly sliced

1 tablespoon grated peeled fresh ginger

1¹/₂ tablespoons soy sauce

1 tablespoon rice vinegar (not seasoned)

1 teaspoon sesame oil

Grated zest of 1 lime

Salt and pepper

1 pound ground pork

¹/₄ cup panko or dried breadcrumbs

TIP: If you happen to have Magic Miso-Mayo in the fridge, try brushing some on top of the meatballs before baking; it transforms into a tasty glaze.

TIP: We often double the recipe and freeze half the meatballs either raw or cooked (see Tip on page 141). If you're cooking them first, let them cool before placing in the freezer. To serve, defrost overnight in the refrigerator. Cook raw ones as detailed above. Heat cooked ones in the oven or microwave.

SAUSAGE AND WHITE BEAN GRATIN

SERVES 6

There's a lot of wiggle room in this hearty crowd-pleaser. You can cook the sausage and bean mixture a day or two in advance (just allow for extra oven time since it will be cold). If you have an ovenproof pan, such as a cast-iron skillet, you can also use that for the entire recipe. Folding some spinach into the mixture before baking is an easy way to add some color and vegetables, but you can skip it or use other leafy greens, such as Swiss chard, escarole, or broccoli rabe (sturdier ones will need to be blanched first). The gratin also reheats well.

—Preheat the oven to 425°F, with a rack in the middle position. In a small bowl, combine the panko and butter, season with salt, and set aside.

—In a large skillet, heat the oil over high heat until it shimmers. Add the sausages and cook, stirring often and breaking up the meat, until browned, about 4 minutes. Leaving as much oil in the pan as possible, transfer the sausage to a medium bowl and set aside.

—Reduce the heat to medium-low, add the onions and garlic and cook, stirring occasionally, until the onions are softened, about 8 minutes. Add the tomato paste and thyme and stir for about 30 seconds. Add the wine and briskly simmer, scraping up any caramelized bits from the bottom of the pan, until almost evaporated, about 2 minutes.

—Add the broth and bring to a simmer, then add the beans, cooked sausage, and any juices. Season with salt and pepper and simmer, stirring occasionally, until heated through and some of the liquid is absorbed, about 5 minutes. The mixture should be wet, but not drowning in liquid. Off the heat, stir in the spinach (if using). Check the seasonings, then transfer the mixture to a 3-quart baking or gratin dish.

—Top evenly with the panko mixture and bake until bubbling and the top is golden brown, about 15 minutes. Let rest for 5 to 10 minutes before serving.

2/3 cup panko or regular dried breadcrumbs

2 tablespoons unsalted butter, melted

Salt

2 tablespoons olive oil

1 pound sweet Italian sausages, casings removed

1 small yellow onion, chopped

4 garlic cloves, minced

1 heaping tablespoon tomato paste

1 scant tablespoon fresh thyme leaves or 1 scant teaspoon dried

1/2 cup dry white wine

1 1/2 cups low-sodium chicken broth

Two 15.5-ounce cans white beans, such as cannellini or Great Northern, drained and rinsed

Pepper

4 large handfuls of baby spinach (optional)

EGGS, MEATLESS, RICE, AND A PIZZA

HUEVOS RANCHEROS

SERVES 4

This may be a traditional Mexican farm breakfast, but we're fans of serving eggs anytime, especially when they're cooked in a lively tomato sauce spiked with jalapeño and lime juice. Serve with warm tortillas (we use them like a utensil to scoop up the huevos and sauce), toast, or brown rice. You can also add an extra egg or two to the pan, if you like.

2 tablespoons olive oil

1 small yellow onion, finely chopped

3 garlic cloves, minced

1 jalapeño, seeded (leave the seeds in for a hotter effect) and finely chopped

One 28-ounce can whole, peeled tomatoes

$^{1}/_{2}$ teaspoon ground cumin

$^{1}/_{4}$ cup water

Salt and pepper

Fresh lime juice

4 large eggs

$^{1}/_{2}$ cup shredded sharp cheddar cheese (about 2 ounces)

Warm small flour tortillas (see Tip, page 32, for warming info), toast, or brown rice

Sour cream (optional)

Handful of cilantro, roughly chopped (optional)

Lime wedges (optional)

—In a large high-sided sauté pan with a lid, heat the oil over medium heat. Add the onions, garlic, and jalapeños and cook, stirring occasionally, until the onions are softened, about 6 minutes. Add the tomatoes and their juices, crushing the tomatoes with your hands or a potato masher (see note, page 118), cumin, and water and season with salt and pepper. Simmer, stirring occasionally, until slightly thickened, about 5 minutes. Add a splash of lime juice, then check the seasonings.

—Crack the eggs into the tomato sauce, spacing them evenly apart. Reduce the heat and gently simmer, covered, until the whites are set and the yolks are cooked to your liking, about 2 minutes for runny eggs. Uncover and top with the cheese. Serve with the warm tortillas, toast, or rice, along with sour cream, cilantro, and lime wedges, if you like.

CRUSTLESS BROCCOLI AND CHEDDAR QUICHE

MAKES ONE 10-INCH QUICHE

The chicest mom Kathy knew growing up (think Jackie O with a platinum bob) made a version of this dish. That was in the '70s, when quiche was all the rage, but in our minds, it defies trend. She was a busy woman, so she skipped the crust and often baked the filling in individual rame-kins in advance. When dinnertime rolled around, she'd warm a few in the oven and pull out some Italian bread for an effortless and popular meal.

Aside from blanching the broccoli, the quiche can be assembled in minutes. If you prefer to use frozen broccoli, there's no need to blanch it; just thaw and pat dry.

——Preheat the oven to 350°F, with a rack in the middle position. Butter a 10-inch glass pie dish, then set aside.

——Bring a large pot of water to a boil over high heat and season it generously with salt; it should taste like seawater. When it returns to a boil, add the broccoli and gently boil, stirring once or twice, until just crisp-tender, 1 to 2 minutes. Drain, rinse with cold water, then thoroughly pat dry and scatter over the bottom of the pie dish. Scatter the cheese evenly over top.

——In a 1-quart measuring cup (see Tip) or medium bowl, whisk together the milk, cream, eggs, nutmeg, 1 teaspoon salt, and pepper to taste until smooth, then pour over the cheese. Bake until the custard is just set in the center, 35 to 40 minutes. (Don't worry if the center is a little trembly; it will cook a little more as it rests.) Let cool slightly before serving.

Unsalted butter for greasing the pie dish

Salt

3 cups small broccoli florets (from about 1 large head of broccoli)

1 cup shredded cheddar cheese (about 4 ounces)

1 cup whole milk

$^2/_3$ cup heavy cream

6 large eggs

Pinch of nutmeg, preferably freshly grated

Pepper

TIP: For convenience, we use a 4-cup measuring cup to measure all of the ingredients for the quiche, ending with the custard, which we whisk right in the cup. First, measure the broccoli, then the cheese. Next, measure the 1 cup milk, add enough cream to reach 1$^2/_3$ cups, then add the eggs, nutmeg, salt, and pepper. Whisk together, then pour the custard into the dish.

BLACK BEAN AND BUTTERNUT SQUASH ENCHILADAS

SERVES 4

The combination of black beans and butternut squash wrapped in tortillas and baked under a blanket of smoky tomato sauce and cheddar is a good choice for Meatless Mondays. To help get dinner on the table even faster, we often use packaged cubed butternut squash, instead of cutting it ourselves, and make the filling a day or two in advance.

2 cups cubed butternut squash

2 cups Everyday Black Beans (page 188) or one 15.5-ounce can black beans, drained and rinsed

2 tablespoons unsalted butter, softened

Grated zest of 1 lime, plus 1 tablespoon juice

Salt and pepper

8 corn tortillas

One 14.5-ounce can crushed tomatoes

¼ cup olive oil

1 chipotle chile in adobo sauce, minced (remove the seeds for a milder effect)

1 tablespoon honey

2 tablespoons water

2 cups shredded sharp cheddar cheese (about 8 ounces)

—Preheat the oven to 350°F, with a rack in the middle position. In a medium saucepan, combine the squash with enough cold water to cover by about 1 inch. Bring to a boil over high heat, then reduce the heat and gently boil until tender, about 6 minutes. Drain the squash and return to the pot. Add the beans, butter, and lime zest. Mash until just a little chunky, then season with salt and pepper. Set the bean mixture aside.

—Spread the tortillas out on a sheet pan and heat in the oven until warmed through, but not toasted, about 4 minutes (if they get crisp, they will crack when you try to roll them). Set aside, leaving the oven on.

—Meanwhile, prepare the tomato sauce. In a medium bowl, combine the tomatoes, oil, chipotles, honey, water, and lime juice, then season with salt and pepper.

—Lightly cover the bottom of a 13 x 9-inch baking dish with some of the tomato sauce. Dip each toasted tortilla in the remaining tomato sauce, then spoon on one-eighth of the bean mixture and roll up. Arrange the filled tortillas in the baking dish seam-side down, cover with the remaining tomato sauce, and top with the cheese. (If all 8 tortillas can't fit across the pan, tuck the last one in crosswise.) Bake until the enchiladas are heated through and the cheese has melted, about 25 minutes, then serve.

 TIP: For an extra-smoky touch, try using fire-roasted canned tomatoes (diced or crushed) in place of the regular crushed ones.

CRISPY TOMATO AND CHEESE QUESADILLAS

SERVES 4

No weeknight cook should be without a trusty quesadilla recipe. This all-purpose one can be served as is or embellished with shredded roast chicken, crumbled chorizo, cooked shrimp, or sautéed leafy greens, including our Basic Swiss Chard (page 149). Toasting the tortillas before adding the filling may be unusual, but this simple technique has a big payoff: It transforms the quesadillas from floppy to crispy. To save time, toast the tortillas in one pan while preparing the filling in another.

—In a large skillet, heat the oil and butter over medium heat, swirling the pan once the butter's melted, until the butter starts to brown. Add the onions and garlic and cook, stirring occasionally, until the onions are softened, about 6 minutes. Add the tomatoes and cook, stirring occasionally, until they start to break down and release their juices, about 3 minutes. Add the vinegar, scraping up any caramelized bits from the bottom of the pan. Stir in the herbs, season with salt and pepper, and set the tomato filling aside.

—Meanwhile, to toast the tortillas, heat a large skillet over medium heat. Add 1 tortilla and cook until lightly toasted with some light brown spots, about 1 minute. Flip the tortilla over and cook until lightly toasted but still pliable, less than 1 minute. Transfer the finished tortilla to a cutting board and repeat with the remaining tortillas. Reserve the pan for cooking the quesadillas and reduce the heat to medium-low.

—Spread one-fourth of the tomato filling over 1 tortilla. Top evenly with one-fourth of the cheese, then place another tortilla on top. Brush the top of the quesadilla with oil and sprinkle with salt. Add the quesadilla to the pan, oiled-side down. Gently flatten it a bit with a spatula and cook until golden, about 2 minutes. Brush the top of the quesadilla with oil, sprinkle with salt, then carefully flip it over. Cook until golden and the filling has melded together, about 2 minutes more.

—Transfer the quesadilla to the cutting board, and repeat with the remaining quesadillas (you can assemble them as the first one cooks). Cut the finished quesadillas into wedges and serve with salsa and sour cream, if you like.

2 tablespoons olive oil, plus extra for brushing on the tortillas

2 tablespoons unsalted butter

1 yellow onion, finely chopped

2 garlic cloves, minced

2 pints cherry tomatoes, halved

1/4 cup red wine vinegar

Handful of cilantro or flat-leaf parsley, chopped

Salt and pepper

8 medium flour tortillas

1 cup shredded sharp cheddar cheese (about 4 ounces)

Charred Tomato Salsa (page 221) or your favorite jarred salsa (optional)

Sour cream (optional)

EXPAT FRIED RICE

SERVES 4

When Kathy told her friend Ginny about this cookbook and the kind of dishes we planned to include, she immediately offered up her fried rice recipe. A single mom and news editor who worked and traveled in Asia for more than 20 years, she knows a thing or two about getting a fast, fuss-free meal on the table.

She uses leftover meat or fish (salmon is a favorite)—but you can also start with raw and cook it in the pan before you add the rice. The thyme is an unusual addition that Ginny calls a delicious accidental discovery. What's more, she felt compelled to clarify two things: It's oyster sauce, not soy sauce, that belongs in fried rice (otherwise, it's like a "salt lick"), and don't just serve it for dinner; it makes a great weekend breakfast.

¼ cup vegetable oil

1 small yellow onion, finely chopped

4 cups cooked rice (see Tip)

2 large eggs

1½ cups bite-size pieces cooked meat or fish

2 cups packed baby spinach, 1 cup cooked small broccoli florets, or ½ cup frozen peas, thawed

Leaves from 2 sprigs thyme

3 tablespoons oyster sauce, plus extra, if needed

—In a wok or large skillet, heat the oil over high heat until it shimmers. Add the onions and cook, stirring often, until they start to brown but are still crisp, about 1 minute. Add the rice and heat through, breaking up any chunks and mixing the grains with the oil and onions, about 2 minutes.

—Crack the eggs onto the rice and cook until almost set, stirring to break up the yolks and coat the rice, about 1 minute. Add the meat or fish and vegetables and heat through, stirring often, about 2 minutes. Add the thyme and oyster sauce and cook for about 1 minute more, stirring often. Check the seasonings, adding salt or more oyster sauce if needed, then serve hot.

TIP: Fried rice is best made with cooked short- or medium-grain rice (not long-grain or coverted rice) that's at least a day or so old and cold. The moisture in freshly cooked, warm rice will result in a gummy texture. Ginny's recipe charmingly called for "yesterday's rice you'd otherwise throw away," but if all you have is just-cooked rice, spread 4 cups of it on a sheet pan, let it cool on the counter, then, depending on how fast you need it, put it in the refrigerator or freezer until cold. Another idea is to order extra rice when you get Chinese takeout and make the fried rice in the next few days.

PIZZA SALAD

SERVES 4 TO 6

Caroline first saw the combination of a warm crispy pizza crust topped with a vinegary chopped salad at an Italian grocery store in her old neighborhood. The pairing was so obvious— and delicious—she couldn't believe she'd never thought of it before. Topping the pizza with slices of prosciutto or flakes of oil-soaked tuna fish makes it more substantial for dinner, but it's great meatless and "fishless," too.

You can make your own dough, but we generally pick up a ball at the local pizzeria or super-market. Because it's more pliable and easier to shape in the pan when at room temperature, we recommend putting it in a large oiled bowl, covering it with plastic wrap or a dish towel, and set-ting it on the counter for about 1 hour (or up to 9 hours) before you use it.

—Preheat the oven to 500°F, with a rack in the upper third position. In a large bowl, combine the shallots and vinegar, then set aside. Grease an 18 x 13-inch sheet pan with oil, making sure you get into the corners. Put the dough on the pan and firmly push and stretch it with your fingers, letting it rest briefly every few pushes and stretches, until it covers the bottom of the pan in a relatively even layer. (Depending on the temperature and elasticity of your dough, it might not stretch as easily. Don't worry if it doesn't completely reach the edges. Just fill the pan as much as you can.) Repair any holes by pinching the dough together.

—Brush the dough with the 2 tablespoons oil. Sprinkle the thyme evenly over the dough, press the leaves into it a bit, and season with salt and pepper. Bake the dough, rotating the pan halfway through, until golden brown on the bottom and the edges start to pull away from the sides of the pan, about 10 minutes.

—Meanwhile, to the bowl with the shallots and vinegar, add a splash of lemon juice and the remaining 3 tablespoons oil. Season with salt and pepper, then whisk together. Check the seasonings by quickly dipping in a piece of lettuce, shaking it off, and tasting. Top the dressing with the tomatoes, artichoke hearts, cucumbers, capers, lettuce, and tuna (if using) and set aside without tossing.

—When the crust is ready, transfer it to a cutting board. Toss the salad, check the seasonings, then mound it evenly over the crust, leaving a narrow border around the edges. Lay the prosciutto slices (if using) across the salad and scatter the feta over top. Cut the pizza salad and serve right away.

1 shallot, minced

2 tablespoons red wine vinegar

2 tablespoons olive oil, plus 3 tablespoons, and extra for greasing the pan

1 ball store-bought pizza dough, at or close to room temperature (see note above)

Leaves from 4 sprigs thyme or 1 scant teaspoon dried

Salt and pepper

Fresh lemon juice

1/2 pint cherry tomatoes, halved

One 6-ounce jar marinated artichoke hearts (about 1 cup), drained and roughly chopped

1 small cucumber, halved lengthwise and thinly sliced

2 tablespoons capers, rinsed

6 large handfuls of assorted lettuces, torn into bite-size pieces

One 5-ounce can tuna packed in oil, drained, or 1/4 pound thinly sliced prosciutto (optional)

1/2 cup crumbled feta cheese (about 2 ounces)

PASTA

ONE-BOWL SUMMER SPAGHETTI

SERVES 4 TO 6

On a hot, lazy day, it's hard to beat this pasta, which involves little more than chopping a few ingredients. The "sauce" can also be made up to about 4 hours ahead of time and left covered on the counter—just omit the mozzarella and add it when you boil the pasta water. We recommend using the best ingredients possible: Local, in-season tomatoes and quality cheese, olives, and olive oil make all the difference.

2 pounds tomatoes (about 3 large), chopped and juices reserved

³/₄ pound fresh mozzarella, cut into ¹/₂-inch dice

1 cup kalamata olives, pitted and roughly chopped

3 garlic cloves, minced

Large handful of basil leaves, roughly torn

¹/₂ cup olive oil, plus extra, if needed

Salt and pepper

1 pound spaghetti

—Bring a large pot of water to a boil over high heat. Meanwhile, in a large bowl, combine the tomatoes and their juices, mozzarella, olives, garlic, basil, and oil. Season generously with salt (the tomatoes, mozzarella, and noodles will soak it right up), add some pepper, then set the tomato mixture aside.

—When the water boils, season it generously with salt; it should taste like seawater. When it returns to a boil, add the pasta, quickly stir to separate the noodles, then cover the pot. When the water returns to a boil again, uncover and boil the pasta until al dente, stirring occasionally. Drain the pasta, then pour it on top of the tomato mixture.

—Let it sit for a couple minutes to warm the mixture, then toss to combine. There should be enough liquid to coat the pasta and form a puddle at the bottom of the bowl. If not, add a little more oil; cooking water may dilute the flavor of the simple sauce too much. Check the seasonings. Divide the pasta among plates or shallow bowls (see Tip below), breaking up any large clumps of cheese with your fingers. Top with the juices at the bottom of the bowl and serve.

TIP: Servings of long pasta varieties, such as spaghetti, fettuccine, and linguini, look so much better when purposefully mounded rather than unceremoniously plopped. Commonplace at restaurants, this flourish (see photo, page 17) is simple to do and only takes a sec. Using tongs, gently grab about half a portion of pasta from the mixing bowl or pan. Bring it over to the plate or shallow bowl, hold the tongs so the pasta rests on the surface, then turn your wrist almost a half turn away from you and release the pasta. Repeat one more time on top of that mound, admire for a sec, then mangia!

TIP: Although pitted olives are convenient to use in this dish, they can be mushy because their inner flesh has been exposed to the brine. As such, we usually opt for unpitted ones. To pit them, put them in a single layer on a cutting board and firmly press down on them with the side of a chef's knife or the bottom of a small pan until they split open. Use your fingers to pull out the pits. Or, for a nicer presentation, skip the pressing and use a paring knife to cut the flesh off of the pits lengthwise into about three slices (see the olives in the photo).

PENNE WITH BROCCOLI RABE, GARLIC, AND CRUSHED RED PEPPER FLAKES

SERVES 4 TO 6

Kathy first had this pasta during a staff lunch at Manhattan's Restaurant Daniel in 1998. Then-chef de cuisine Alex Lee whipped up a big batch in minutes, and it was devoured just as quickly. After some persuading, he shared his recipe with Kathy (albeit in chef's shorthand), and it has become one of her go-to weeknight pasta dishes, not least because it's as effortless and tasty as it is full of leafy greens.

Salt

1 large bunch of broccoli rabe (about 1 pound), stems cut into 1-inch pieces and leaves cut crosswise into 2-inch ribbons

1 pound penne

1/3 cup olive oil, plus extra, if needed

4 garlic cloves, smashed

Large pinch of crushed red pepper flakes

Freshly grated Parmesan or pecorino cheese

—Bring a large pot of water to a boil over high heat and season it generously with salt; it should taste like seawater. When it returns to a boil, add the broccoli rabe and gently boil, stirring once or twice, until just tender, about 2 minutes. Reserving the water in the pot, transfer the rabe to a medium bowl, pour off any excess water, and set aside.

—When the water returns to a boil, add the pasta, quickly stir to separate the noodles, then cover the pot. When the water returns to a boil again, uncover and boil the pasta until al dente, stirring occasionally.

—Meanwhile, in a large high-sided sauté pan, heat the oil, garlic, pepper flakes, and a large pinch of salt over medium heat. Cook, tilting the pan so the garlic is surrounded by the oil, until the garlic is fragrant and just starting to turn golden, about 3 minutes.

—Add the blanched broccoli rabe (watch for any spattering) and about 1/2 cup of the water from the pasta pot and cook, stirring occasionally and squishing the stem pieces a bit, until heated through and combined, about 2 minutes. Check the seasonings (it should taste a little salty and spicy) and set aside.

—When the pasta is ready, drain it, pour it on top of the broccoli mixture, then toss to combine over medium heat. If the pasta looks dry, add a little more oil. Check the seasonings and serve with a generous amount of the cheese.

TIP: Blanching usually helps tame broccoli rabe's bitterness, but if you find yourself with a particularly strong bunch (usually because it is old or was picked late), add a couple pats of butter with the olive oil at the end to smooth out the flavor.

PASTA RAGS WITH ROCK SHRIMP AND CHERRY TOMATOES

SERVES 4 TO 6

This dish shows off the delicate texture of no-boil lasagna noodles (Barilla is our preferred brand) in an unusual way. We break up the noodles in the style of maltagliati; *Italian for "badly cut," the name refers to the odds and ends left over after making pasta. Tender, sweet rock shrimp are a particularly good match for the silky pieces of pasta, but you can also use regular shrimp. Top the pasta with toasted, seasoned breadcrumbs or panko (see DIY Breadcrumbs, page 120) for another layer of flavor and texture.*

—Bring a large pot of water to a boil over high heat. Meanwhile, break up each pasta sheet into about 6 pieces roughly the same size. When the water boils, season it generously with salt; it should taste like seawater. When it returns to a boil, add the pasta, quickly stir to separate the noodles, then cover the pot. When the water returns to a boil again, uncover and boil the pasta until al dente, stirring occasionally.

—Meanwhile, in a large high-sided sauté pan, heat the oil, garlic, pepper flakes, and a large pinch of salt over medium heat. Cook, stirring occasionally, until the garlic is fragrant and just starting to turn golden, about 2 minutes. Add the shrimp and cook, stirring often, for 1 minute. Raise the heat to high, add the wine and tomatoes, and simmer, stirring occasionally, until the shrimp are almost cooked through, about 2 minutes for rock shrimp and about 3 minutes for regular shrimp. Off the heat, stir in the butter and lemon zest. Check the seasonings (it should taste a little salty and spicy) and set aside.

—When the pasta is ready, drain it, reserving about 1 cup of the cooking water, then pour the noodles on top of the shrimp mixture. Add a little more oil and the parsley and toss to combine over medium heat. If the pasta looks dry, add some of the cooking water. Check the seasonings and serve.

One 9-ounce package no-boil lasagna noodles

Salt

$1/4$ cup olive oil, plus extra for finishing the dish

3 garlic cloves, thinly sliced

Large pinch of crushed red pepper flakes

1 pound rock shrimp or medium shrimp, peeled and deveined (if using medium shrimp, cut into bite-size pieces)

$1/2$ cup dry white wine

1 pint cherry tomatoes, halved

2 tablespoons unsalted butter

Grated zest of 1 lemon

Large handful of flat-leaf parsley, roughly chopped

TOP **6** DINNER-RELATED COMMENTS

While planning and writing this cookbook, one of our unofficial hobbies was to record memorable weekday meal-related quotes from friends and family members. No matter how much—or little—time you spend at the stove, these sentiments of dread, hope, and confusion will probably sound familiar.

1. "So, WHAT'S FOR DINNER?"

—MIKE, FOOLISH HUSBAND, JOURNALIST, AGE 46

Asked expectantly by Kathy's husband less than 1 minute after arriving home from work—with the household in full meltdown mode. It would be tempting to bonk any spouse who does this with a pan and then say something along the lines of "I'm outta here!" before driving to the local tavern for a beer and a burger. Actually, that's exactly what one should do. And if it happens again, put him or her in charge of dinner for the next few nights.

2. "WHY IS COOKING SO HARD?"

—NICHOLE, COUSIN, FARMING APPRENTICE, AGE 25

Nichole gets a mild panic attack every time she even thinks about facing the stove; hence, she lives off of a diet of tofu, hummus, and almond butter. When she told Caroline about her cooking anxiety, her response was not to recommend a sedative, but to share her own kitchen disaster stories (pushing hair out of her face while seeding fiery chiles bare-handed and having both eyes swell shut; having the blender explode while pureeing hot soup). Caroline then suggested the following: Pick a simple dish that Nichole loved to eat—like a vegetable omelet—learn how to make it, and prepare it repeatedly until she didn't need a recipe. Having just one "back-pocket" dish can go a long way toward building confidence in the kitchen.

3. "I'LL COOK ANYTHING IF SOMEONE WOULD JUST TELL ME WHAT TO MAKE."

—PAM, FRIEND, MOM, AND VOLUNTEER, AGE 51

Declared in a moment of exasperation by a friend who's actually an enthusiastic and skilled cook, but felt overwhelmed by so many recipes and so little time ("I entered the words 'chicken breast' into Google and 687,540 recipes came up!"). This sentiment helps remind us that even people who know their way around a kitchen still like a little friendly direction ("Make *this* chicken breast recipe; it's great because . . .") So when in doubt, or overwhelmed by choice, ask for help. Chances are that sending an SOS to friends and relatives for a foolproof and delicious chicken recipe will yield results. This is also a terrific use of Facebook.

4. "BY THURSDAY NIGHT I'VE RUN OUT OF THINGS TO MAKE. . . . "

—FELICIA, NEIGHBOR, STAY-AT-HOME MOM, 43

Said with resignation on suffering from menu-planning fatigue. At this point, we'd refer her to the recipes in *Keepers*. Then again, we'd never judge if she served any of the following for dinner: microwave popcorn, cereal (out of the box), or a banana and an ice cream sandwich, a fallback meal once referred to by a friend and mom of a 3-year-old as "dinner and dessert." Bonus: no cooking and no dishes.

5. "ARE YOU PUTTING GINGER IN THAT?"

—TIM, ANOTHER FOOLISH HUSBAND, TRADER, AND NONCOOK, 41

You may have to cook for people who have some restrictions, not the allergy kind, more like the "you know I don't like cilantro/dark meat/couscous/squash" type of issues. Caroline's husband thinks he doesn't like ginger. Little does he know that she cooks with it ALL THE TIME. If you're the cook, don't feel like you need to share and vet every ingredient you're using. Sometimes children AND adults think they don't like something . . . but they actually do.

6. "WHY BOTHER COOKING WHEN I CAN DO TAKEOUT OR MICROWAVE A FROZEN DINNER?"

—MEGAN, FRIEND, SOMETHING TO DO WITH THE INTERNET, 33

This may seem like a hard argument to win because of course it's faster and easier to push buttons on your phone or microwave to get dinner on the table. But unless you have the means to order from a 4-star restaurant, takeout will rarely taste better than the dishes you make yourself; neither will nuked ones. Plus, when you're the "chef," you know exactly how much salt, fat, sugar, and preservatives are in your food; you can tweak the dish to your taste; you're probably saving money and helping save the planet (think of all those plastic and Styrofoam containers); you're setting a positive example for any little ones in the house; and you won't have pesky soy sauce packets clogging up your junk drawer.

SPAGHETTI WITH 10-MINUTE BASIC TOMATO SAUCE

SERVES 4 TO 6

If you normally rely on jarred tomato sauces, here are five reasons to make this sauce instead the next time spaghetti is on the menu: It's fresher tasting, preservative-free, less expensive, requires only basic pantry items, and takes barely any more effort or time.

We find the quality of canned whole tomatoes is generally better and more consistent than the crushed version, so we usually buy the former. Caroline crushes them into the pan using her hands; Kathy prefers to crush them against the bottom of the pan with a potato masher. Either way, pierce them first to avoid spurts and remove any hard cores. Sometimes canned tomatoes can be very acidic; if you find this to be the case when you taste the sauce, add a pinch of sugar.

Salt

1 pound spaghetti

2 tablespoons olive oil, plus extra for finishing the dish

2 large garlic cloves, minced

One 28-ounce can whole, peeled tomatoes

Handful of basil leaves, roughly torn (optional)

Freshly grated Parmesan or pecorino cheese

—Bring a large pot of water to a boil over high heat and season it generously with salt; it should taste like seawater. When it returns to a boil, add the pasta, quickly stir to separate the noodles, then cover the pot. When the water returns to a boil again, uncover and boil the pasta until al dente, stirring occasionally.

—Meanwhile, in a large high-sided sauté pan, heat the oil, garlic, and 2 large pinches of salt over medium heat. Cook, stirring occasionally, until the garlic is fragrant and just starting to turn golden, about 2 minutes. Add the tomatoes and their juices, crushing the tomatoes with your hands or a potato masher (see note above). Bring the mixture to a boil, then reduce the heat and simmer until you can draw a line through it with a wooden spoon and it doesn't fill in immediately, 5 to 7 minutes. The sauce should be light and fresh tasting, so don't let it cook down too much. Check the seasonings (it should taste a little salty) and set aside.

—When the pasta is ready, drain it, reserving about 1 cup of the cooking water, then pour the noodles on top of the tomato sauce. Add a little more oil and toss to combine over medium heat. If the pasta looks dry, add some of the cooking water. Check the seasonings, add the basil (if using), and serve with the cheese.

TIP: Once you know how to make a basic tomato sauce, you can easily turn out a number of variations, including **Spicy Tomato-Cream Sauce** (opposite page); **puttanesca** (add some minced anchovy fillets with the garlic and capers and chopped olives with the tomatoes); and **Amatriciana** (cook some chopped bacon or pancetta and then onion before the garlic and add a generous amount of black pepper and crushed red pepper flakes). You can also cook the basic sauce down a little more and use it on pizza.

TIP: If you prefer a smooth sauce rather than a chunky one, instead of crushing the tomatoes, puree them with a handheld blender (right in the can, if you like and are careful).

ANGEL HAIR PASTA WITH SPICY TOMATO-CREAM SAUCE

SERVES 4 TO 6

There's something about the combination of this light cream sauce (a variation on the 10-Minute Basic Tomato Sauce on the opposite page) and delicate angel hair pasta that makes us swoon, but the sauce marries well with other types of pasta, too. If you don't like heat, omit the crushed red pepper flakes.

—Bring a large pot of water to a boil over high heat. Meanwhile, in a large high-sided sauté pan, heat the oil, garlic, pepper flakes, and 2 large pinches of salt over medium heat. Cook, stirring occasionally, until the garlic is fragrant and just starting to turn golden, about 2 minutes. Add the tomatoes and their juices, crushing the tomatoes with your hands or a potato masher (see note, opposite page). Bring the mixture to a boil, then reduce the heat and simmer until you can draw a line through it with a wooden spoon and it doesn't fill in immediately, 5 to 7 minutes. The sauce should be light and fresh tasting, so don't let it cook down too much. Stir in the cream and bring to a simmer. Check the seasonings (it should taste a little salty) and set aside.

—When the water boils, season it generously with salt; it should taste like seawater. When it returns to a boil, add the pasta, quickly stir to separate the noodles, then cover the pot. When the water returns to a boil again, uncover and boil the pasta until al dente, stirring occasionally.

—Drain the pasta, reserving about 1 cup of the cooking water, then pour the noodles on top of the tomato sauce. Add the parsley and a large splash of the cooking water and toss to combine over medium heat. If the pasta looks dry, add some more of the cooking water. Check the seasonings and serve with the cheese.

2 tablespoons olive oil

2 large garlic cloves, minced

Very large pinch of crushed red pepper flakes

One 28-ounce can whole, peeled tomatoes

$1/2$ cup heavy cream

Salt

1 pound angel hair pasta

Large handful of flat-leaf parsley, chopped

Freshly grated Parmesan or pecorino cheese

DIY BREADCRUMBS

It may sound odd to call breadcrumbs trendy, but converting loaves into tiny pieces has seemingly become the scrapbooking of the culinary world—a quaint and rediscovered activity that can be oddly addictive. It's a worthwhile one, though: Homemade breadcrumbs are almost always tastier than store-bought, are simple to prepare, and are economical, particularly if you're using leftover bread you would otherwise throw away.

There are two categories of breadcrumbs: fresh (made from fresh bread) and dried (made from stale bread or fresh breadcrumbs that are dried out). We make both, but generally stick to dried because they keep better and are a little more versatile. Use them to thicken sauces and soups; bind meatballs (see Italian Wedding Soup, page 141, and Our Favorite Meat Loaf, page 86); coat fish and chicken before cooking (see Fish Fingers with Lime-Ginger Dipping Sauce, page 36, and Deviled Panko-Crusted Chicken Thighs, page 45); and top baked stuffed vegetables, casseroles, and gratins (see Tomato and Zucchini Gratin, page 164).

But as easy as it is to make homemade breadcrumbs, when you're in the middle of a recipe, it's even easier to reach for a bagful that you prepared in advance. To ensure you always have a stash, make a big batch, store it in the freezer, and replenish it as needed. Here's our method for plain dried breadcrumbs and a toasted, seasoned variation:

We're partial to round country loaves, but any type of seedless bread, or combination of breads, will do. Cut it into large pieces. If the bread's not already stale, set them aside, unwrapped and at room temperature, until they're dried out. This can take a day or two. (You can also dry out the bread in a 250°F oven, turning once; depending on the type of bread and size of the pieces, it may take 15 to 45 minutes. Let cool completely before proceeding.) Whiz the pieces in the food processor until coarse crumbs form. You can process them until fine, if you prefer, but we like them with a little more texture. Transfer the breadcrumbs to a resealable freezer bag, pushing out any excess air, and store in the freezer for up to 6 months. There's no need to thaw before using.

For extra-crunchy breadcrumbs with a savory edge, in a large skillet, heat 1 tablespoon olive oil or unsalted butter over medium heat, then add 1 cup dried breadcrumbs. Cook, stirring often, until golden, about 3 minutes, then season with salt and pepper. (Adjust the amounts as needed, but don't crowd the pan too much.) Toasted, seasoned breadcrumbs are wonderful sprinkled over pastas (see Fusilli with Zucchini, Gruyère, and Breadcrumbs, opposite page), cooked vegetables (see Green Beans with Sun-Dried Tomato Pesto Breadcrumbs, page 165), soups, and even simply prepared meats and fish. Depending on what you're pairing them with, you can also flavor them with lemon zest, dried or fresh chopped herbs, minced garlic, grated Parmesan cheese, crushed red pepper flakes. . . . They're best used within a day or so.

Note that the light and flaky Japanese breadcrumbs called panko are a wonderful alternative to dried breadcrumbs (particularly store-bought breadcrumbs). We actually prefer them for preparations where we want an extra-crispy crust, as in the Fish Fingers on page 36. They can also be toasted and seasoned as detailed above. (We don't recommend the preseasoned versions.)

FUSILLI WITH ZUCCHINI, GRUYÈRE, AND BREADCRUMBS

SERVES 6

Slightly caramelized zucchini, sweet onions, and nutty Gruyère topped with toasted bread-crumbs makes a great side dish. Add some pasta and you've got an even better main course. Take the time to properly salt and squeeze the zucchini before you cook it; this process removes excess moisture so that the zucchini won't be soggy or mushy when you cook it, and that makes a big difference to the finished dish.

—Bring a large pot of water to a boil over high heat. Meanwhile, put the shredded zucchini in a colander set in the sink, sprinkle with 2 teaspoons salt, and toss to combine. Let drain while the water comes to a boil, occasionally squeezing the mixture firmly to remove excess moisture. Before you cook the pasta, give the zucchini one last good squeeze, removing as much moisture as possible, then set aside.

—When the water boils, season it generously with salt; it should taste like sea-water. When it returns to a boil, add the pasta, quickly stir to separate the noodles, then cover the pot. When the water returns to a boil again, uncover and boil the pasta until al dente, stirring occasionally.

—Meanwhile, in a large high-sided sauté pan, heat the butter over medium heat, swirling the pan once it's melted, until it starts to brown. Add the onions, anchovy paste, and pepper flakes and cook, stirring occasionally, until the onions are softened and starting to carmelize, about 8 minutes.

—Raise the heat to medium-high and add the drained zucchini. Cook, stirring occasionally, until tender and it begins to brown around the edges, about 3 minutes. Add a big splash of lemon juice and scrape any caramelized bits from the bottom of the pan. Season with salt and pepper (it should be a little salty) and set aside.

—When the pasta is ready, drain it, reserving about 1 cup of the cooking water, then pour the noodles on top of the zucchini mixture. Drizzle with oil, add a large splash of the cooking water and the cheese, then toss over medium heat until the cheese starts to melt. If the pasta looks dry, add some more of the cooking water. Check the seasonings and serve topped with the toasted breadcrumbs.

2½ pounds zucchini (about 5 medium), shredded

Salt

1 pound fusilli or rotini

2 tablespoons unsalted butter

1 yellow onion, finely chopped

½ teaspoon anchovy paste

Large pinch of crushed red pepper flakes

Fresh lemon juice

Pepper

Olive oil for finishing the dish

½ cup shredded Gruyère cheese (about 2 ounces)

1 cup toasted, seasoned dried breadcrumbs (see DIY Breadcrumbs, opposite page)

RIGATONI WITH SWISS CHARD PESTO

SERVES 4 TO 6

If you have a container of Swiss Chard Pesto (recipe follows) in the fridge or freezer, just boil some pasta and dinner is ready. Alternatively, you can make the pesto in the time it takes to cook the noodles. And there's so much green in this dish that we count it as a serving of vegetables, too. That's our kind of weeknight meal.

—Bring a large pot of water to a boil over high heat. Season the water generously with salt; it should taste like seawater. When it returns to a boil, add the pasta, quickly stir to separate the noodles, then cover the pot. When the water returns to a boil again, uncover and boil the pasta until al dente, stirring occasionally.

—Drain the pasta, reserving about 1 cup of the cooking water, then transfer the noodles to a large bowl. Add the pesto, a drizzle of oil, and a large splash of the cooking water, and toss to combine. If the pasta looks dry, add some more of the cooking water. Check the seasonings and serve with the cheese.

Salt

1 pound rigatoni

1 cup Swiss Chard Pesto (recipe follows)

Olive oil for finishing the dish

Freshly grated pecorino or Parmesan cheese

SWISS CHARD PESTO MAKES ABOUT 1²/₃ CUPS

As great as traditional basil pesto is, it's not the only kind of pesto. Parsley, spinach, sun-dried tomatoes, and even carrot tops can also be used to make pesto—and, unlike the big, fragrant bunches of basil available in the summer, are abundant year-round. You can also sub out the standard pine nuts and Parmesan cheese, which are wonderful but costly ingredients. We particularly like the combination of Swiss chard, cilantro, sunflower seeds, and pecorino; it complements everything from pasta to roast chicken to a grilled cheese sandwich.

Swiss chard stems and ribs are too fibrous for the pesto, but rather than throw them away, sauté them in some olive oil and eat them or use them in a soup or vegetable stock.

—In a food processor, combine the Swiss chard, garlic, lemon zest, a big splash of lemon juice, 2 large pinches of salt, and some pepper. Pulse a few times to combine, pushing down the chard as needed. Add the sunflower seeds and cilantro and pulse until finely chopped. With the machine running, add the oil in a slow stream and process until incorporated. Add a little more oil, if needed. Transfer the pesto to a medium bowl, stir in the cheese, then check the seasonings.

—If you're not using the pesto right away, cover the top with a thin layer of olive oil. The pesto will keep, covered in the refrigerator, for about 1 week. It can also be frozen for up to 1 month; just omit the cheese and add it before using.

3 well-packed cups green Swiss chard leaves (stems and center ribs removed), torn into large pieces

3 garlic cloves

Grated zest of 1 lemon, and juice

Salt and pepper

¹/₃ cup toasted sunflower seeds

Handful of cilantro

²/₃ cup olive oil, plus extra, if needed

1 cup freshly grated pecorino or Parmesan cheese

FARFALLE WITH GORGONZOLA, HAM, AND PEAS

SERVES 4

If you've had a rough week, something a little decadent for dinner can be a mood-changer. But while this dish is unquestionably luxurious, it is actually one of the simplest pasta preparations we know. If you're not a "blue cheese person," rest assured the flavor of the Gorgonzola mellows once it's combined with the cream. And if you're serving vegetarians, you can offer the ham on the side for anyone who wants it.

Salt

1 pound farfalle or orecchiette

1 cup heavy cream

¼ pound Gorgonzola cheese

1 cup frozen green peas, thawed

¼ pound sliced ham (baked French or Black Forest ham is nice)

Coarsely ground black pepper (see note, page 190)

—Bring a large pot of water to a boil over high heat. Season the water generously with salt; it should taste like seawater. When it returns to a boil, add the pasta, quickly stir to separate the noodles, then cover the pot. When the water returns to a boil again, uncover and boil the pasta until al dente, stirring occasionally.

—Meanwhile, in a large high-sided sauté pan, heat the cream and cheese over medium heat. Simmer, stirring often and breaking up the cheese, until the mixture is smooth and slightly thickened, about 3 minutes. Add the peas and cook until warmed through, about 1 minute. Off the heat, shred the ham into the pan and stir. Check the seasonings (the sauce should be a little salty, but since the cheese and ham are salty, extra salt may not be needed) and set aside.

—When the pasta is ready, drain it, reserving about 1 cup of the cooking water, then pour the noodles on top of the sauce. Toss to combine over medium heat. If the pasta looks dry, add some of the cooking water. Check the seasonings and serve topped with pepper.

TIP: When cooking tubular or short pasta shapes like penne or farfalle, we often remove it from the pot with a type of handheld strainer called a spider. It works like a charm and saves us from having to wash a crevice-y colander or trying to fit the bulky vessel in the dishwasher. We also don't miss lugging the hot, heavy pot to the sink and having our faces steamed when we drain it. Another benefit: If you need any cooking water to moisten the sauce, it's right there on the stove. Adding some cooking water also helps to "marry" the pasta with the sauce.

KALE CARBONARA

SERVES 4 TO 6

A lot of people we know are reluctant to make traditional carbonara because they're wary about consuming raw eggs or they've had problems turning the eggs into a silky sauce, scrambling them instead. Our version sidesteps both of those issues: We poach the eggs so that the whites are cooked but the yolks are still runny enough to help form the sauce. The addition of onions and kale might make an Italian balk (we sometimes serve the pasta with bowls of lemon wedges and dried breadcrumbs, too), but all we can say is that they make for a worthy spin-off of the original dish.

1 tablespoon olive oil, plus extra for finishing the dish

1 small yellow onion, chopped

5 ounces bacon (about 5 slices), cut crosswise into $1/3$-inch pieces

3 large garlic cloves, sliced

Large pinch of crushed red pepper flakes

1 bunch of slightly damp kale (about $3/4$ pound), stems and center ribs removed, and leaves torn into large pieces

Salt and pepper

1 pound fettuccine, spaghetti, or bucatini

4 large eggs

1 cup freshly grated Parmesan or pecorino cheese, plus extra for serving

—Bring a large pot of water to a boil over high heat. Meanwhile, in a large high-sided sauté pan with a lid, heat the oil over medium heat. Add the onions, bacon, and garlic and cook, stirring occasionally, until the onions are soft and the bacon fat is rendered, about 10 minutes. Add the pepper flakes and stir until fragrant, about 30 seconds. Add the kale and cook, stirring often, until softened, about 3 minutes. Season with salt and pepper (it should taste a little salty) and set aside.

—Season the boiling water generously with salt; it should taste like seawater. When it returns to a boil, add the pasta, quickly stir to separate the noodles, then cover the pot. When the water returns to a boil again, uncover and boil the pasta until al dente, stirring occasionally.

—When the pasta is almost ready, spread the kale mixture in an even layer in the pan. Make 4 "nests" in the kale an equal distance apart, then crack an egg into each. Add enough of the pasta water, pouring it in against the side of the pan, to almost cover the kale. Cover the pan and poach the eggs over medium-low heat until the whites are just set and the yolks are still runny, about 3 minutes. Set aside.

—Drain the pasta, reserving about 1 cup of the cooking water, then pour the noodles on top of the eggs. Add a little more oil and the cheese and toss to combine. If the pasta looks dry, add some more of the cooking water. Check the seasonings and serve with more cheese.

LEMONY TURKEY BOLOGNESE

SERVES 4 TO 6

This is a lighter, leaner, brighter, and much faster alternative to the classic long-simmered beef Bolognese. We prefer to use dark turkey meat; it's moister and more flavorful than white meat. If you can't find it, a combination of white and dark is the next best choice. For an extra citrus note, add a splash of lemon juice when you toss the pasta with the sauce.

—Bring a large pot of water to a boil over high heat. Meanwhile, in a large high-sided sauté pan, heat the butter over medium heat, swirling it once it's melted, until it starts to brown. Add the pancetta and cook, stirring occasionally, until it begins to crisp around the edges, about 4 minutes. (If using bacon, there will be more rendered fat; pour off all but 1 tablespoon or so.) Add the onions, garlic, oregano, and pepper flakes and cook, stirring occasionally, until the onions are softened, about 5 minutes.

—Raise the heat to high and add the turkey. Cook, stirring often and breaking up the meat, until the meat is browned, about 5 minutes. Add the tomato paste and stir for about 1 minute. Add the wine and briskly simmer, scraping up any caramelized bits from the bottom of the pan. Reduce the heat, stir in the yogurt and lemon zest, and gently simmer to meld the flavors, about 5 minutes. Check the seasonings (it should taste a little salty) and set aside.

—Meanwhile, season the boiling water generously with salt; it should taste like seawater. When it returns to a boil, add the pasta, quickly stir to separate the noodles, then cover the pot. When the water returns to a boil again, uncover and boil the pasta until al dente, stirring occasionally.

—Drain the pasta, reserving about 1 cup of the cooking water, then pour the pasta on top of the Bolognese sauce. Drizzle with oil, add the cheese, and toss to combine over medium heat. If the pasta looks dry, add some of the cooking water. Check the seasonings and serve with more cheese.

1 tablespoon unsalted butter

4 ounces pancetta or bacon (about 4 slices), finely diced

1 yellow onion, finely chopped

2 garlic cloves, minced

2 teaspoons dried oregano

Small pinch of crushed red pepper flakes

1 1/2 pounds ground turkey, dark meat or a combination of dark and white

1 heaping tablespoon tomato paste

1/2 cup dry white wine

1 cup Greek yogurt

Grated zest of 1 lemon

Salt

1 pound rigatoni or penne

Olive oil for finishing the dish

1/2 cup freshly grated Parmesan or pecorino cheese, plus extra for serving

SKILLET LASAGNA

SERVES 6

Most lasagnas involve a big investment of time and a sink full of pots and pans, but not this one. It has all the pleasures of lasagna—layers of tender noodles, homemade meat sauce, deliciously gooey cheese—but can be whipped up in less than an hour using a single skillet. We're fans of Barilla's no-boil lasagna noodles (see Pasta Rags with Rock Shrimp and Cherry Tomatoes, page 115), but feel free to use whatever brand you like.

—In a large high-sided sauté pan with a 3-quart capacity and a lid, heat the oil over high heat until it shimmers. Add the sausages and cook, stirring often and breaking up the meat, until browned, about 4 minutes. Leaving as much oil in the pan as possible, transfer the sausage to a medium bowl and set aside.

—Reduce the heat to medium-low, add the onions, garlic, and pepper flakes to the pan, and cook, stirring occasionally, until the onions are softened, about 7 minutes. Add the oregano, the tomatoes and their juices, crushing the tomatoes with your hands or a potato masher (see note, page 118), the sprig of basil, and the cooked sausage and any juices. Season with salt and pepper, then gently simmer for 5 minutes, stirring occasionally. Check the seasonings (it should be a little salty) and discard the basil sprig.

—Break half of the lasagna noodles in half crosswise (it's fine if smaller pieces break off) and as you do so, push each piece into the sauce under the sausage, distributing them evenly throughout the pan. Break the remaining half of the noodles in half and distribute them evenly over the sauce, then push down on them with the back of a spoon to submerge them. Cover the pan and gently simmer (raising the heat a little, if needed) until the noodles are tender and the sauce has thickened slightly, about 12 minutes.

—Dollop the mascarpone over the lasagna and swirl it into the sauce. Top with the mozzarella and gently simmer, covered, until the cheese is melted, about 2 minutes. Off the heat, top with the basil leaves, tearing any large ones. Let the lasagna rest, uncovered, for about 10 minutes, then serve.

2 tablespoons olive oil

1 pound sweet or hot Italian sausages, casings removed

1 small yellow onion, finely chopped

4 garlic cloves, minced

Large pinch of hot red pepper flakes

1 teaspoon dried oregano

Two 28-ounce cans whole, peeled tomatoes

1 sprig basil, plus a handful of basil leaves

Salt and pepper

One 9-ounce package no-boil lasagna noodles

4 ounces mascarpone cheese or cream cheese (1/2 cup)

1/2 pound fresh mozzarella, thinly sliced and patted dry

TIP: The next time you end up with a crusty or blackened skillet or pot (it happens to everyone), don't sigh and reach for the scouring pad. Just add an inch or so of water and briskly simmer until the stuck-on or burned bits soften and start to come away from the bottom. After the water cools, wash as usual. For real doozies, add a big splash of distilled white vinegar to the water before boiling; after draining the cooled water, scrub with baking soda, then wash. It should be (almost) as good as new. We usually start the process before we sit down for dinner, so by the time we're ready to clean up, the pan is cool enough to handle.

SOUPS AND TOASTS

CHILLED PEA SOUP WITH MINT

SERVES 6

This soup is spring in a bowl. Since fresh peas are a fleeting seasonal treat, we reach for reliably sweet—and convenient—frozen peas here, and elsewhere, without hesitation. If you want to twirl things up a bit, garnish each bowl with some crabmeat or a few cooked shrimp (perhaps splurging on precooked ones for ease) paired with diced cucumbers, julienned radishes, and/or thinly sliced chives. Even better, toss the additions first with a little olive oil, lemon juice, salt, and pepper. You can also serve the soup hot, if you like.

1 tablespoon unsalted butter

1 small yellow onion, finely chopped

5 cups low-sodium chicken broth

6 cups frozen peas (about 28 ounces), preferably the "baby sweet" variety

Salt and pepper

1 cup lightly packed mint leaves

$^{1}/_{2}$ cup heavy cream or plain Greek yogurt (optional)

—In a large pot, heat the butter over medium-low heat. Add the onions and cook, stirring often, until softened, about 8 minutes. Add the broth, raise the heat to high, and bring to a boil. Add the peas, season with salt and pepper, and stir. Cover the pot, bring the broth back to a boil, and cook only until the peas are thawed (overcooking will dull the color), 2 to 3 minutes. Stir in the mint.

—Working in batches, process the soup in a blender until smooth and pass through a strainer set over a large bowl, pushing on the solids with a ladle until all of the liquid is extracted. Discard the solids. (It's not necessary to strain the soup, but doing so gives it a silkier texture.)

—Refrigerate until cold, stirring occasionally so that it chills evenly and doesn't discolor in places. If the soup is too thick after it chills, thin it with a little broth or water. Check the seasonings, then serve drizzled with the heavy cream or dolloped with the yogurt, if you like. The soup will keep, covered in the refrigerator, for about 2 days.

TIP: To preserve the peas' vivid color, work quickly to avoid letting them sit in the hot broth too long before processing in the blender. For a really vibrant-looking soup, immediately put the container of soup in an ice bath (a mixture of water and ice in a bowl) after processing, stirring often until it is cool. But don't worry if your soup does turn more of an army green; that won't affect its flavor.

AS-YOU-GO TOMATO SOUP WITH QUINOA

SERVES 6

We call this "as-you-go" because it's the kind of dish that is very easy to step away from without consequence while you manage whatever other household activities are swirling around you. Simply turn off the heat and pick up where you left off when you're ready. In the end, you'll still have a bright-tasting, herb-infused, creamy soup that's perfect on its own or alongside a grilled cheese sandwich.

Use just one herb or different combinations depending on what you like and have on hand (tarragon and basil would be great choices). Tomato soup is often seen with rice, but we prefer quinoa, which has a grainy nuttiness and is also very healthful. Spoon it into the bowls before adding the soup so it's like a little discovery.

½ cup quinoa, rinsed

1 cup low-sodium chicken broth or water

Salt

2 tablespoons olive oil, plus 2 tablespoons

1 yellow onion, chopped

2 carrots, chopped

2 celery stalks, chopped

3 garlic cloves, chopped

Leaves from 4 sprigs thyme

Leaves from 1 sprig rosemary, chopped

2 cups water

Two 28-ounce cans whole, peeled tomatoes

Pepper

Fresh lemon juice

—In a very small saucepan, combine the quinoa, broth, and a pinch of salt, and bring to a boil over high heat. Reduce the heat, stir once, and simmer, covered, until tender and the liquid is absorbed, about 15 minutes. Let rest, covered, for about 5 minutes, then fluff the quinoa with a fork and set aside.

—Meanwhile, in a large pot, heat 2 tablespoons of the oil over medium heat. Add the onions, carrots, celery, and garlic and cook until the onions are softened, about 10 minutes. Add the thyme and rosemary and cook until fragrant, about 30 seconds. Add the water and scrape up any caramelized bits from the bottom of the pot. Add the tomatoes and their juices, crushing the tomatoes with your hand into the pot, and season with salt and pepper. Simmer, partially covered and stirring occasionally, until the vegetables are soft and the tomatoes have cooked down a bit, about 10 minutes.

—Add the remaining 2 tablespoons oil and blend the soup with an immersion blender until smooth. (If you don't have an immersion blender, use a standard blender and process the soup in batches.) Add a splash of lemon juice, then check the seasonings. Add a few spoonfuls of cooked quinoa to the bottom of each bowl, ladle the soup on top, and serve.

TIP: If the soup is acidic, which is sometimes the case depending on the brand and/or type of tomatoes you use, stir in a little sugar to balance it, if you like. Be careful not to overdo it; the soup shouldn't be sweet.

WATER WORKS

The problem with cooking school is that it's easy to get caught up in the world of elaborate, labor-intensive preparations: puff pastry, seafood mousses, lobster reductions. You learn how to make them, you practice on your family, and then you start to feel like it's sacrilege to bake a tart at home with store-bought dough. That's pretty much where Kathy was the night she attended a stocks and sauces demo taught by the legendary André Soltner, the former chef-owner of New York's Lutèce and a dean of her culinary school, the International Culinary Center, also in the city.

The demo was interesting, but what she really wanted to know was what stocks Chef Soltner used in his home kitchen to make soups and sauces. Surely, he always had some brown veal or chicken stock on hand, maybe even a container of duck stock. She waited until after class when there were only a few stragglers around before nervously posing her question. His answer floored her: "Stocks?" he laughed good-naturedly, his tall toque somehow managing to stay put as he threw his head back. "What's wrong with water?"

Sensing her surprise, and maybe disappointment, he quickly added that stocks were wonderful and important to his restaurant dishes, but that at home he mostly cooked with water. "Look," he explained, brown eyes gleaming, "you can make a perfectly nice soup with water. And if you have nice *sucs* [the caramelized bits] in your pan, then deglaze with wine, simmer with some water, finish with a little butter, and you will have a nice sauce for your meat or fish."

For Kathy, it was a liberating moment (and proceeded to free up a lot of her time), but it took a while for her to realize the bigger lesson he had taught her. Of course he knew that water wouldn't give you the same richness, or body, or flavor that stock will. (In this book, we usually split the difference and go with low-sodium broth.) But ultimately, good cooking is not about fancy ingredients, or slavishly following recipes, or relying on certain provisions. It's about working with what you have, making the most of it, and being flexible. Kathy didn't say it then—she recalls a much more sheepish exit—but wants to now: *Merci beaucoup*, Chef Soltner.

SHRIMP WONTON SOUP

SERVES 6

This may not sound like the kind of soup you can put together on a weeknight, but Kathy's neighbor Lihong showed us otherwise. Store-bought wonton skins and canned chicken broth are conveniences she adopted after moving to the States from China. She also likes the flavor olive oil lends. We modified her version a bit so you can get all the ingredients from your supermarket and rely on the speed of your food processor (Lihong chops the wonton filling with two large cleavers!). The wontons are also great on their own, served with soy sauce or a combo of about 2 parts soy sauce, 1 part Chinese black vinegar (substitute balsamic vinegar, if you like), and a splash of sesame oil and/or chile oil.

There are lots of ways to fold wontons, traditional and not (see page 138 for three examples). We detail one of the prettier styles below and on page 138, but simply forming triangles by folding them in half is really fast and easy and yields a very delicate wonton because there are so few overlaps of dough. Do what you're most comfortable with and what you have time for. You can also make the wontons ahead of time and freeze them raw for up to a month or so. (For details on how to freeze the wontons, see the Tip on freezing meatballs for the Italian Wedding Soup, page 141.)

WONTONS

½ **pound medium shrimp, peeled, deveined, spread out on a dish, and put in the freezer until they just start to firm up, about 15 minutes**

¼ **packed cup water chestnuts, rinsed, dried, and roughly chopped**

1 teaspoon finely chopped peeled fresh ginger

1 scallion (white and pale green part only), sliced

½ **tablespoon olive oil**

¼ **teaspoon salt**

⅛ **teaspoon pepper, preferably white**

About 30 square white or yellow wonton wrappers

—For the wontons: In a food processor, combine the shrimp, water chestnuts, ginger, and scallions and pulse until the shrimp are finely chopped but not pureed. Transfer to a bowl and stir in the oil, salt, and pepper.

—Fill a small dish with cold water and line a sheet pan with plastic wrap or parchment paper. Lay 3 wonton wrappers on a work surface (keeping the remaining wrappers covered with a damp paper towel) and put a rounded teaspoon of the shrimp filling in the center of each. Dip a brush or forefinger in the water and run it around the edges of each wrapper. Be sure to moisten the entire perimeter or the wonton will have leaks. Fold each wrapper in half on the diagonal to form a triangle. Seal the edges, pressing out any excess air from around the filling.

—Next (you can skip this step, if you like), curl and fold the two bottom-side corners back toward each other so they overlap and point upward, then moisten and press together. Put each wonton on the sheet pan and repeat with the remaining wrappers and filling. Refrigerate until needed.

—In a large pot, bring 4 quarts of water to a boil.

— Meanwhile, for the soup: In a medium saucepan, combine the broth, ginger, and garlic and simmer for 10 minutes. Discard the ginger and garlic, then stir in the soy sauce and sesame oil. Check the seasonings, adding salt if needed. Cover and keep the soup hot while you cook the wontons.

— Add the wontons to the boiling water in two batches, give them a quick stir, and cover the pot. When the water returns to a boil, remove the lid and gently boil, stirring occasionally, until the wontons are just cooked through, about 3 minutes. Using a strainer or spider, portion the wontons into bowls. Ladle the hot soup over the wontons and serve hot.

SOUP

8 cups low-sodium chicken broth

Two 1-inch pieces of fresh ginger, smashed

1 garlic clove, smashed

2 tablespoons soy sauce

1 tablespoon sesame oil

Salt

TIP: When we're feeling like we need a hit of greens, we add a few handfuls of baby bok choy, spinach, or snow peas to the broth just before serving; gently boil until just tender. You can also cook the wontons in the broth, but the flour from the wrappers affects the clean taste and makes it cloudy, so we generally avoid it. There's the risk of "dirtying" it with leaked filling, too.

IT'S A WRAP

— Lay 3 wonton wrappers on a work surface and put a rounded teaspoon of the shrimp filling in the center of each.

— Moisten the perimeter of each wrapper with water, fold into a triangle, and seal the edges, pressing out any air.

— If you like, fold the 2 bottom-side corners over and across the wonton so they overlap (see the first 3 wontons on the left, above), then moisten and press together.

— Or, as explained on page 136, you can choose to curl and fold the 2 bottom-side corners back toward each other so they overlap and point upward (see the wontons at the back of the tray, above), then moisten and press together.

LENTIL AND CHORIZO SOUP

SERVES 6

This rich, deeply flavored soup is a great choice whenever there's a chill in the air. After some minimal chopping and sautéing, there's little to do except wait for the lentils to soften. We often prepare the vegetables in the morning to make the process even easier, or double up on cooking one night, then refrigerate the soup so it's ready to go later in the week. It tastes even better when the flavors have had time to mingle, and it also freezes well. A drizzle of good olive oil on top of the soup in the bowls is really nice; a grating of Parmesan is, too.

2 tablespoons olive oil

1 onion, finely chopped

2 carrots, halved lengthwise and chopped

2 celery stalks, halved lengthwise and chopped

3 garlic cloves, smashed

1 tablespoon tomato paste

1 teaspoon ground cumin

$^{1}/_{2}$ pound brown lentils (about 1$^{1}/_{4}$ cups), rinsed and picked over

8 cups low-sodium chicken broth

4 ounces Spanish chorizo, casing removed, halved lengthwise, and sliced on the diagonal

$^{1}/_{2}$ tablespoon apple cider vinegar

Large handful of flat-leaf parsley or cilantro, roughly chopped (optional)

Salt and pepper

—In a large pot, heat the oil over medium heat. Add the onions, carrots, celery, and garlic and cook, stirring often, until the onions are softened, about 10 minutes. Add the tomato paste and cook, stirring often, for about 1 minute.

—Add the cumin and lentils and cook, stirring often, for about 1 minute. Add the broth and bring the soup to a boil over high heat. Reduce the heat and simmer, stirring occasionally, until the lentils are almost tender, about 30 minutes. Add the chorizo and cook until the lentils are tender, about 5 to 10 minutes more. Stir in the vinegar and herbs (if using) and check the seasonings. Depending on the flavor of the broth and the chorizo, you may not need to add salt or pepper. Serve hot.

 TIP: If you prefer a thicker, more stewlike soup, simmer it for an extra 20 minutes or so, adding the chorizo at the end. The lentils will break down and more of the liquid will evaporate, further concentrating the flavor.

ITALIAN WEDDING SOUP

SERVES 6

Loaded with tender meatballs, silky spinach, and tiny pasta shapes, this soup is a favorite in both our households. Once you make the meatballs, it takes only a few minutes to finish, so set yourself up for an effortless future meal by preparing a double batch of the meatballs and freezing half raw (see Tip). You're already measuring and mixing, so the only additional work is rolling out the extra meatballs.

Many supermarkets carry premixed packs of "meatball" or "meat loaf" meat, a combination of ground beef, pork, and veal. If yours doesn't, use one-third of each or half beef and half pork.

—In a large pot, combine the broth and garlic and briskly simmer for about 5 minutes.

—Meanwhile, in a medium bowl, beat the egg. Add the cheese, onion, milk, oregano, garlic powder, ½ teaspoon salt, and a large pinch of pepper and stir together. Add the meat and panko and gently mix together with a fork or your hands. (The mixture will be a little "wet" and soft.)

—Shape the meat mixture into about thirty 1-inch-diameter balls and put on a plate. When all the meatballs are ready, bring the broth back to a simmer, carefully drop them into the broth and simmer, stirring occasionally, until cooked through, 3 to 5 minutes.

—Add the pepper flakes and cooked pasta and heat through, then stir in the spinach and cook until just wilted. Check the seasonings, adding salt and pepper if needed, and serve hot.

8 cups low-sodium chicken broth

2 garlic cloves, smashed

1 large egg

¼ cup freshly grated Parmesan or pecorino cheese

2 tablespoons grated yellow onion and juices (grated on the medium holes of a box grater)

2 tablespoons whole milk

¼ teaspoon dried oregano

⅛ teaspoon garlic powder

Salt and pepper

½ pound "meatball" or "meat loaf" meat (see note above)

2 tablespoons panko or dried breadcrumbs

Pinch of crushed red pepper flakes

¾ cup acini de pepe or ditalini pasta, cooked in boiling salted water until al dente

6 large handfuls of baby spinach

TIP: You can cook the pasta in the chicken broth, but it's tricky to time with the meatballs and makes the broth cloudy, so we prefer to do it separately. You can also cook the pasta up to 2 days in advance and refrigerate it, covered.

TIP: To freeze the meatballs, put them in the freezer on a parchment paper–lined tray; once they're frozen, seal them in a freezer bag and write the name and date on the bag. They'll keep for about 2 months. There's no need to thaw the meatballs before adding to the broth, but they will take longer to cook.

TOASTS

EACH VARIETY MAKES ABOUT 4 SERVINGS

Yes, toast for dinner. We serve it all the time. Why? Because any variation on an open-faced sandwich is a creative way to turn the odds and ends in your fridge and pantry into a tasty and easy meal. The possibilities are endless, but here are our favorites. Each recipe should yield enough for four people, but you can adjust them to make more, or less if you want to serve a few varieties at one time. For a meal, we usually serve two types.

We like to use an Italian, sourdough, or rustic country loaf cut into ¹/₂-inch-thick slices, but any bread is fine. Pop it in the toaster, grill it, or toast it in the oven at 350°F for about 8 minutes (we usually set the slices on a sheet pan fitted with a wire rack). For extra-tasty toasts, butter the slices before adding the toppings.

TOAST FOR DINNER? YES! WE SERVE IT ALL THE TIME. WHY? WHY NOT!

1. MELTED CHERRY TOMATOES WITH GOAT CHEESE AND BASIL In a large skillet, melt **1 tablespoon unsalted butter** over medium heat. When the foam has subsided, add **1 pint cherry tomatoes** and cook until the tomatoes soften, gently pressing down on them to release some of their juices. Add **¹/₄ teaspoon anchovy paste** and cook 1 minute more, then season with **salt** and **pepper.** Slather some **goat cheese** on the toasts and top with the tomatoes and torn **basil leaves.**

2. WARM PEAS WITH HERBS AND GREEK YOGURT Boil **2 cups frozen peas** (or fresh shelled peas) in generously salted water until just cooked through, about 2 minutes, then drain and pat dry. While still warm, season them with a healthy drizzle of **olive oil,** a squeeze of **fresh lemon juice,** and **salt** and **pepper.** Put a spoonful of **whole-milk Greek yogurt** on the toasts and top with the peas and some chopped **flat-leaf parsley** or **mint leaves.**

3. CANNELLINI BEANS AND PESTO Drain a **15.5-ounce can of cannellini beans,** rinse the beans, and pat dry. In a medium skillet, warm them over medium heat with some **olive oil, red wine vinegar, grated lemon zest,** and **smoked paprika,** then season with **salt** and **pepper.** Spoon the beans on the toasts, mashing them down a bit, and top with a spoonful of **pesto,** such as Swiss Chard Pesto (page 123) or a store-bought variety.

4. SUN-DRIED TOMATO OMELET AND ARUGULA Lightly beat **4 large eggs,** then chop and add **4 drained oil-packed sun-dried tomatoes.** Season with **salt** and **pepper.** In a small skillet, heat **¹/₂ tablespoon olive oil** over medium heat. Add the eggs and cook until they start to set, then lift up an edge and let any uncooked egg run underneath. When the eggs are just set, fold the omelet in half, let cook for a few more seconds, then slide it onto a cutting board and cut crosswise into thin strips. Toss a handful of **arugula** with a little **olive oil, balsamic vinegar, salt,** and **pepper,** put on the toasts, and top with the omelet strips.

5.   AVOCADO WITH RADISHES AND LIME Rub the toasts with the cut side of $\frac{1}{2}$ **garlic clove.** Peel, halve, and remove the pit from **2 avocados,** then scoop some of the flesh onto each toast and mash down a bit. Top with a squeeze of fresh **lime juice,** a few thin slices of **radish,** and a sprinkle of **salt.**

6.   SMOKED SALMON AND EGG SALAD Peel and roughly chop **4 warm hard-boiled large eggs** and stir in **1 heaping tablespoon Dijon mustard, 1 shallot** finely chopped, some chopped **fresh herbs** of your choice, and a glug of **olive oil,** then season with **salt** and **pepper. Butter** the toasts, then top with some **smoked salmon (about 4 slices total),** a squeeze of **fresh lemon juice,** and some of the egg salad.

7.   CHORIZO AND AIOLI Mince **1 large garlic clove,** stir together with $\frac{1}{3}$ **cup mayonnaise,** and set the aioli aside. Slice **6 ounces Spanish chorizo.** In a medium skillet, heat $\frac{1}{2}$ **tablespoon olive oil** over medium heat. Add the chorizo and cook until heated through and crisp. Spread the aioli on the toasts and top with the chorizo and some roughly chopped **flat-leaf parsley** (optional).

8.   CREAMED MUSHROOMS WITH TARRAGON Thinly slice **1 pound mushrooms** (button, cremini, shiitake, and/or chanterelle, if you're feeling fancy). In a large skillet, heat **2 tablespoons olive oil** over medium heat. Add **1 large shallot,** minced, and cook until softened, then raise the heat to medium-high. Add the mushrooms, season with **salt** and **pepper,** and cook until browned and any moisture has evaporated. Add $\frac{1}{4}$ **cup white wine** and briskly simmer, scraping up any caramelized bits from the bottom of the pan, until it's almost evaporated. Stir in $\frac{1}{3}$ **cup heavy cream** and simmer until slightly reduced. Add some chopped **fresh tarragon** and check the seasonings. Spoon the mushrooms on the toasts.

9.   SMASHED BROCCOLI WITH LEMON AND PECORINO Cut $\frac{1}{2}$ **head of broccoli** into small florets and boil in generously salted water until tender. Drain, then pat dry. Add a healthy drizzle of **olive oil,** a squeeze of **fresh lemon juice,** and some grated **lemon zest** and freshly grated **pecorino cheese.** Season with **salt** and **pepper** and stir gently to combine. Top the toasts with the broccoli, mashing it down a bit, then sprinkle with **smoked paprika** (optional).

10.   CURRIED CHICKEN AND MANGO SALAD Dice **1 cooked boneless, skinless chicken breast** (leftover roast or rotisserie chicken is fine). Dice **1 mango** and add to the chicken. Add $\frac{1}{4}$ **cup mayonnaise,** $\frac{1}{4}$ **cup Greek yogurt,** $\frac{1}{4}$ **teaspoon mild curry powder,** and about **1 tablespoon fresh lime juice.** Season with **salt** and **pepper** and stir gently to combine. Top the toasts with the salad and sprinkle with chopped **chives** (optional).

VEGETABLES

SKILLET ASPARAGUS

SERVES 4

This technique for cooking asparagus is based on one we discovered years ago in an issue of Cook's Illustrated. When we first read it, it didn't sound right because it involved cooking the asparagus over high heat past the crisp-tender stage. But after trying it, we were sold. Any woodiness in the stalks disappears, the flesh becomes succulent, the flavors concentrated. It's now our default asparagus-cooking mode. For an extra flourish, drizzle a little balsamic vinegar or fresh lemon juice over the spears before serving.

2 tablespoons olive oil

1 pound medium or large asparagus

Salt and pepper

—In a large skillet with a lid, heat the oil over medium-high heat until it shimmers. Add the asparagus in a single layer, cover, and cook for 5 minutes, gently agitating the pan a few times while holding down the lid.

—Uncover, turn the asparagus over, and season with salt and pepper. Cover again and cook, occasionally agitating the pan, until the asparagus are tender with some browned and crispy spots, 2 to 3 minutes more. Check the seasonings and serve.

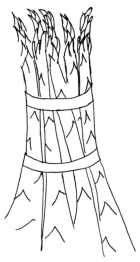

BASIC SWISS CHARD

SERVES 3 OR 4

We often hear from friends that they'd like to eat more dark, leafy greens but find them too bitter or strong-tasting or they don't really know how to prepare them. Yes, those tall, frilly, nutrient-rich bunches can seem foreboding lying on the produce shelf, and, yes, they do have a more assertive flavor than, say, string beans. But they're worth getting to know.

For a side dish, a good place to start is to steam-sauté relatively mild Swiss chard with olive oil and garlic. (Add some crushed red pepper flakes for heat, if you like.) It's an easy preparation that retains the nutrients while softening the flavor. From there, move on to kale or collards. Use the same method, but remove the stems and center ribs and increase the cooking time as needed. (These tougher stems and ribs are generally edible but are better suited to longer cooking soups, stews, or vegetable stocks.)

—In a large skillet with a lid, heat the oil and butter over medium heat. Add the garlic and chard stems and cook, stirring often, until the stems soften, about 3 minutes. Add the chard leaves, season with salt, then reduce the heat to medium-low and cook, covered and stirring occasionally, until the leaves are just tender, 2 to 4 minutes.

—If there's a lot of liquid in the pan, raise the heat and briskly simmer, uncovered, until there are just a few small pools. Check the seasonings and serve.

1 tablespoon olive oil

1 tablespoon unsalted butter

1 large garlic clove, minced

1 bunch of slightly damp Swiss chard (about ³/₄ pound), stems cut into ¹/₂-inch pieces, leaves cut crosswise into 1-inch ribbons (keep the stems and leaves separate)

Salt

TIP: Leaving a little water on the Swiss chard after rinsing it creates steam in the pan that helps cook it.

PARMESAN BROCCOLI

SERVES 4

Broccoli was the only vegetable Caroline would eat when she was a kid (be encouraged, parents of picky eaters, she now eats everything but fish eyeballs), so her mom made this dish at least once a week. The always reliable combination of olive oil, garlic, and crushed red pepper flakes, which works with everything from leafy greens like the chard on page 149 to sautéed zucchini and pasta, gets a boost from grated lemon zest and Parmesan.

Salt

1 large head of broccoli (about 1¼ pounds), cut into small florets

2 tablespoons olive oil

2 garlic cloves, thinly sliced

Pinch of crushed red pepper flakes

Grated zest of 1 lemon, and juice

Freshly grated Parmesan or pecorino cheese

—Bring a large pot of water to a boil over high heat and season it generously with salt; it should taste like seawater. When it returns to a boil, add the broccoli and gently boil, stirring once or twice, until crisp-tender, about 2 minutes. Drain and pat dry.

—In a large skillet, heat the oil, garlic, and pepper flakes over medium heat. Cook, stirring occasionally, until the garlic is fragrant and just starting to turn golden, about 2 minutes. Add the blanched broccoli and cook, stirring often, until coated with the oil and heated through, about 2 minutes. Add the lemon zest and a big splash of lemon juice, season with salt, and toss to combine. Check the seasonings and serve topped with a generous sprinkling of the cheese.

 TIP: There's no need to discard broccoli's hard stalks—they taste great and have more fiber than the florets. Just peel them, cut into chunks, and use as you would the florets, cooking them a little longer if needed. Or you can cut them very thin and eat them raw out of hand, add them to salads, or cut the stems, too, and make a broccoli slaw with the dressings on pages 182 or 211.

WARM CORN SALAD

SERVES 4

This dish and the Raw Corn Salad on page 175 have similar ingredients, but the browned butter and miso paste used here take them in a whole other direction. Adding the milky juices from the corn cobs is key to achieving a rich creaminess, and it only takes a minute to extract them, so don't skip that step: After cutting the kernels from an ear of corn (see Tip), scrape down the bare cob with the dull side of the knife and let the juices run into the kernels.

2 tablespoons unsalted butter

1 small red onion, finely chopped

1 jalapeño, seeded and finely chopped

1 heaping tablespoon white miso paste

3 cups fresh corn kernels (about 5 ears), plus milky juices

Grated zest of 1 lime, and juice

Salt and pepper

—In a large skillet, heat the butter over medium heat, swirling once it's melted, until it starts to brown. Add the onions and jalapeños and cook, stirring occasionally, until softened, about 5 minutes. Add the miso and corn kernels with juices and cook, stirring occasionally (making sure the miso dissolves), until the corn is warmed through, about 3 minutes.

— Add the lime zest and a splash of lime juice, season with pepper, and stir to combine. Check the seasonings (since the miso is salty, salt may not be needed) and serve.

TIP: To minimize stray kernels when cutting corn from the cob, break off the "handle" and hold the ear at a slight angle, with the base set on the bottom of a large, wide bowl or sheet pan. With a serrated knife, cut from the top of the ear down to the base, angling the knife so that you don't cut too deep and remove the hard core with the kernels. Turn the ear a bit and repeat until the cob is bare.

CANDIED CARROTS

SERVES 4

This classic French technique for cooking carrots was one of the first things that Kathy learned in cooking school. It's elemental and elegant, and the carrots wind up tasting like candy. A round of parchment paper (or cartouche) is traditionally used to cover the carrots, helping them cook evenly while allowing moisture to evaporate, but a lid set ajar on the skillet works, too. You can use the same method for other vegetables, such as fennel, turnips, and sugar snap peas.

—In a medium skillet, combine the carrots, enough cold water to barely cover (about 1¼ cups), the butter, sugar, and salt. Bring the liquid to a boil over high heat, then reduce the heat and simmer, partially covered, until the carrots are crisp-tender, about 5 minutes.

—Uncover, raise the heat to high, and cook, tossing occasionally (and more often toward the end), until the liquid has reduced to a clear glaze and evenly coats the carrots, 5 to 7 minutes more. (If the liquid is almost evaporated, but the carrots aren't tender, add a little more water and continue to cook.) Check the seasonings and serve.

1 pound carrots, cut on the diagonal into ¼-inch-thick slices

2 tablespoons unsalted butter

1¹/₂ tablespoons sugar

Very large pinch of salt

TIP: Using a 1,000-stroke-a-minute, jujitsu-like approach to peeling carrots may look impressive, but it isn't very efficient. We've found the quickest and best way to peel a carrot (or similar-shaped vegetable, including a potato) is this: Hold it in the palm of your nondominant hand, with the stem end at your wrist and your fingers cradling the "body" low along the sides. Starting at the stem end, run the peeler down the length of the carrot in one stroke. Use your thumb to rotate the carrot a few degrees toward your forefinger, then run the peeler down the carrot again. Repeat until the entire carrot is peeled. The process may seem awkward at first, but once you get the hang of rotating the carrot in your hand, there's nothing to it.

THE MANY FACES OF GARLIC

It seems like every week the selection of jarred garlic—chopped, crushed, sliced, minced—at our supermarkets grows. We use a lot of garlic and know all too well it can be a pain to prep, particularly in a rush (how many times have we skipped drying our hands completely before peeling cloves and ended up with the papery skins pasted to our fingers?). But while jarred garlic may be convenient, we aren't fans: It generally includes a preservative and other ingredients that affect the flavor and texture.

There are two types of prepared garlic we do like, though: peeled whole fresh cloves (usually found in small bags in the refrigerated produce section) and Dorot brand frozen garlic cubes (labeled as "crushed," although we'd define it as minced), which have minimal additives and can be used frozen or defrosted. Unfortunately, these aren't as widely available as jarred, but that seems to be changing. If buying them seems too frivolous, but you want to simplify your garlic prep/cleanup, here are two options:

- Peel a bunch of cloves at one time and refrigerate them in a plastic bag with any excess air squeezed out. They should last a week or two.

- If you mainly use minced garlic, mince a bunch at one time and refrigerate it in a glass jar covered in olive oil; it should keep for about a week and the resulting garlic-flavored oil is a bonus.

There's actually another type of prepared garlic we like, but it's not raw and we never buy it: roasted whole cloves. Soft, mellow, and slightly sweet, they are delicious slathered on toasted country-style bread or crackers; added to salad dressings, mashed potatoes, dips, hummus, compound butters, and pasta sauces; pureed with hot chicken or vegetable broth for a simple soup—maybe with some raw egg and herbs whisked in and topped with freshly grated Parmesan. Luckily, in addition to being so good and versatile, they couldn't be simpler to make:

Preheat the oven to 375°F, with a rack in the middle position. Working with as many heads as you like (we usually prepare 3 to 5 at a time), cut off just enough of the pointy end to expose the cloves. Put the heads in a baking dish just large enough to hold them. Drizzle with olive oil, season with salt and pepper, then toss to combine. Turn the heads cut side up. Cover the pan with foil and roast until the cloves are tender and golden brown, 35 to 45 minutes. Let cool, then gently squeeze the cloves out of the skins; transfer to a glass jar and cover with olive oil. The roasted garlic will keep, covered in the refrigerator, for up to 2 weeks.

BRAISED BRUSSELS SPROUTS WITH BACON

SERVES 4

Are you a Brussels sprouts refusenik? Are you related to one? Well, this dish may convert you. (The bacon helps.) You can use pancetta or Spanish chorizo in place of the bacon, although you'll probably need to add a little more oil.

—In a large skillet with a lid, heat the oil over medium heat. Add the bacon and shallots and cook, stirring occasionally, until the bacon fat is rendered, about 5 minutes. Pour off all but 2 tablespoons of fat, raise the heat to high, and add the Brussels sprouts, garlic, and thyme. Cook, stirring occasionally, until the Brussels sprouts are lightly browned, about 3 minutes.

—Add the broth, bring to a boil, then reduce the heat and simmer, covered, until the Brussels sprouts are crisp-tender, about 8 minutes. Add the vinegar and continue simmering, uncovered, until the liquid is almost evaporated, about 2 minutes more. Remove the thyme sprigs, then stir in the butter, season with salt and pepper, and serve.

1 tablespoon olive oil

4 ounces bacon (preferably thick-sliced), diced

2 shallots, minced

1 pound Brussels sprouts, halved (or quartered if large)

2 garlic cloves, smashed

2 sprigs thyme

1$\frac{1}{2}$ cups low-sodium chicken broth

2 tablespoons apple cider vinegar

2 tablespoons unsalted butter

Salt and pepper

ROAST YOUR VEGETABLES

Unless it's the height of summer and our ovens are on hiatus, hardly a week goes by in which we aren't roasting a big pan (or two, or three) of vegetables. In our view, nothing enhances their natural sweetness and flavor like a slick of olive oil, a liberal sprinkling of salt, and some high heat. But not only are they delicious on their own, they pair nicely with lots of main courses, make an easy meal when tossed with a salad, grain, or pasta, and are great in sandwiches.

If you prepare a couple batches on a Sunday—and you'll marvel at the almost effort-free results—you'll be set for most of the week. Combine a variety of vegetables (a favorite winter mix is carrots, butternut squash, and parsnips) or, for more flexibility, roast different types individually. Either way, be warned: If you leave the finished vegetables on the stovetop unattended for even a few minutes, they will likely disappear into the mouths of hungry passers-by.

Here's our basic roasting method, which can be used for most vegetables, in any amount:

——**PREHEAT THE OVEN TO 425°F.** (You can go about 25°F higher or lower depending on the type of vegetable and if you prefer them more tender or browned, but this is a good starting point.) We use the middle rack position if we're roasting one pan and the lower and upper thirds if we're roasting two, switching racks halfway through.

——**CUT THE VEGETABLES EVENLY AND NOT TOO SMALL.** Different-size vegetables won't be ready at the same time. We like 1-inch or so pieces, which yield a nice ratio of crispy/caramelized outside to creamy inside and don't end up too small (vegetables shrink as they roast), but you can adjust as you like. There's no need to cut long, thin vegetables like green beans or asparagus, though; just roast them whole. The same goes for cherry tomatoes. They should also be completely dry before they go into the oven; otherwise they will steam and not roast properly.

——**DON'T CROWD THEM.** Make sure they can fit in the pan in a single layer. If they're pressed up against each other like they're at a rave, they'll steam (see above). We usually use an 18 x 13-inch sheet pan, but any low-sided pan is fine.

——**SEASON THEM DIRECTLY ON THE PAN.** No need to dirty a bowl. Our standard recipe is a generous amount of salt (preferably kosher or fine sea salt, although coarse sea salt is fantastic on potatoes), pepper, and enough olive oil to lightly coat each piece. Depending on what we're serving them with or how we're using them (tossed with a grain salad, for instance), we sometimes add various spices and/or herbs before we roast them, including **rosemary, thyme leaves, crushed red pepper flakes, cumin, coriander seeds, turmeric, ground ginger,** or **smoked paprika.**

COMBINE A VARIETY OF VEGETABLES— A FAVORITE WINTER MIX IS CARROTS, BUTTERNUT SQUASH, AND PARSNIPS

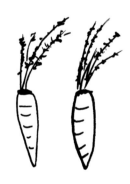

—ROAST THEM. Put the pan in the oven and cook the vegetables until lightly browned on the bottom, about 15 minutes. Toss them (we do this with a sturdy thin-lipped metal fish spatula—see page 12—angling it down toward the bottom of the pan and scraping under the vegetables to get up all the crusty bits, the *best* part), then continue to cook until tender and golden brown in spots or almost all over, with slightly crispy edges. Watch frilly or delicate vegetables like broccoli or string beans closely toward the end of the cooking time so they don't burn. Depending on the type of vegetable and how big the pieces are, this will probably take 10 to 20 minutes more. If the vegetables are almost tender but aren't browning well, raise the heat to 450°F; conversely, if they're browned but not tender, reduce the heat to 375°F.

—EMBELLISH, IF YOU LIKE. You can also combine them with flavorings after roasting (see the following roasted cauliflower, eggplant, and acorn squash recipes). Feel free to add:

- A sprinkle of Parmesan cheese and/or lemon zest
- Some toasted nuts or seeds (or add untoasted ones to the pan 3 to 6 minutes before the vegetables are finished cooking); a handful of golden raisins (particularly nice with cauliflower)
- A splash of vinegar (balsamic on roasted string beans is really good)
- Or, open your pantry and have fun experimenting with your favorite ingredients

Roasted vegetables are generally good hot, warm, and even right out of the fridge. Enjoy!

COOKING WITH ALL THE SENSES

The first time we heard a chef say he could smell when a dish was properly seasoned, we thought he must have had a few glasses of wine with lunch. You need to taste a dish to determine that, right?! Well, some 20 years later, we owe him an apology. Our cooking senses surely aren't as developed as his (he'd toiled in some of the world's best kitchens since he was an adolescent), but they've reached the point where a quick look, listen, sniff, and/or feel can convey almost as much as an actual bite.

It's not a special gift; it's about being attuned to the minutiae of cooking at every stage, from prepping the raw ingredients to serving the finished dish. And doing it over and over and over until it's reflexive. You've heard of muscle memory? Well, this is like sense memory. For instance, Kathy's been known to sweetly call downstairs to turn the burner heat down when her husband is making pancakes. "What do you mean?" he asks. "Everything's fine." Then, a minute later: "Oh. The pancakes burned." It wasn't that she smelled burning pancakes; she smelled browning butter, which meant the heat was too high and would lead to burned pancakes. And she knew this because it'd happened to her numerous times and sometimes still does when she's not paying attention.

A bunch of asparagus spotted languishing in a pan of barely boiling water? Sadly, waterlogged, limp, and army fatigue green is their fate. That pan of oil heard sputtering and crackling furiously at the first dip of battered chicken? The oil's too hot, meaning the coating will probably brown before the meat is cooked. And the steak on the grill that feels really soft and squishy when prodded? It's too rare to take off—unless you like your beef practically mooing.

Now, it's possible to make tasty food without being sensitive to such details (particularly if you cook from well-written, thorough recipes or stick with the tried and true), so why bother to develop your senses in relation to the kitchen? The way we see it, using all five of them when you cook is like taking care of a mischievous child. You have a much better chance of a successful outcome, or bypassing a potential mishap, if all of your antennae are up. "Conor, it's awfully quiet in there . . ." Plus, it will make you a better, more confident cook. We don't know if we'll ever get to the point where we can smell the right amount of seasoning, but that doesn't stop us from trying.

ROASTED CAULIFLOWER DRESSED UP

SERVES 6

Roasting turns pale, mild, underappreciated cauliflower into something earthy, nutty, and irresistible. Try it as a side dish or salad ingredient or stuffed into a warm pita with hummus and black olives. But it's also wonderful dressed up with this vinegary mix of shallots, capers, lemon zest, and parsley.

1 head of cauliflower (about 2$\frac{1}{2}$ pounds), cut into small florets

$\frac{1}{3}$ cup olive oil

Salt and pepper

1 shallot, cut crosswise into thin rings

1 tablespoon white wine vinegar

1 tablespoon capers, rinsed and roughly chopped

Grated zest of 1 lemon

Handful of flat-leaf parsley, roughly chopped

— Preheat the oven to 425°F, with a rack in the middle position. Put the cauliflower on an 18 x 13-inch sheet pan, sprinkle with the oil, and season with salt and pepper. Using your hands, combine well, then spread the cauliflower out across the pan. Roast until lightly browned on the bottom, about 15 minutes, then toss the pieces around, spreading them out again. Roast until tender and golden brown, with slightly crispy edges, about 15 minutes more.

— Meanwhile, in a large bowl, combine the shallots and vinegar and let marinate for at least 20 minutes (and up to 1 hour or so). Just before the cauliflower is ready, add the capers, lemon zest, and parsley to the bowl and stir together. Add the roasted cauliflower and toss to combine. Check the seasonings and serve.

ROASTED EGGPLANT WITH YOGURT SAUCE

SERVES 4

Grilled eggplant may be more common, but it can't compare to velvety, crispy-edged roasted eggplant cubes. Enjoy them plain or paired with this garlicky herbed yogurt sauce. When buying eggplant, look for ones that have smooth, shiny skin and feel heavy for their size, and be sure to give them a tap: They should sound solid, not hollow.

——Preheat the oven to 425°F, with a rack in the middle position. Put the eggplant and garlic on an 18 x 13-inch sheet pan, sprinkle with the oil and cumin, and season with salt and pepper. Using your hands, combine well, then spread the eggplant and garlic out across the pan. Roast until the eggplant is lightly browned on the bottom, about 15 minutes, then toss the pieces around, spreading them out again. Roast until tender and golden brown, with slightly crispy edges, 10 to 15 minutes more.

——Meanwhile, in a small bowl, stir together the yogurt and enough water to thin it a little (about 3 tablespoons). Stir in the lime or lemon zest and honey and set aside.

——When the eggplant is ready, transfer it to plates or a medium bowl, removing the garlic cloves.

——Squeeze the softened garlic from the skins into the yogurt mixture and stir, mashing the garlic as needed, until the sauce is fairly smooth. Stir in the herbs, season with salt and pepper, then check the seasonings. Drizzle some oil over the sauce and serve with the roasted eggplant.

2 pounds eggplant (about 2 medium), cut into 1-inch pieces

6 unpeeled garlic cloves

$^1/_3$ cup olive oil, plus extra for finishing the dish

1 heaping teaspoon ground cumin

Salt and pepper

1 cup Greek yogurt

Grated zest of 1 lime or lemon

$^1/_2$ teaspoon honey

Handful of mixed fresh herbs (such as dill, flat-leaf parsley, chives, tarragon, or cilantro), chopped

TIP: The yogurt sauce is even better the next day, so if you have any extra, spoon it over roasted or grilled fish or chicken, as well as other types of roasted or grilled vegetables, such as cauliflower, zucchini, peppers, portobello mushrooms, or tomatoes.

ROASTED ACORN SQUASH WITH JALAPEÑO-LIME BUTTER

SERVES 4

Never know what to do with acorn squash? Halve a couple, season the cut sides, and throw them in a 400°F oven. About 40 minutes later, the golden flesh is soft, sweet, slightly caramelized, and ready to eat. We like it just fine with a big pat of butter (and another generous sprinkle of salt and pepper), but it's awfully good with this jalapeño-lime butter, too.

Like most compound butters—which are ideal for adding lots of flavor with minimal effort— it will keep well in the freezer for about 2 months so long as it's tightly covered, so we usually make a quadruple batch and portion it into small ramekins or plastic containers. (You can also roll up the butter in parchment paper logs; this yields nice slices later, but we find the process a little fussy.) Use it wherever you want a spicy, citrusy, buttery touch.

2 small acorn squash (about 1½ pounds each), halved lengthwise and seeded

Olive oil for coating the squash

Salt and pepper

4 tablespoons unsalted butter, softened

1 garlic clove, minced

1 to 2 tablespoons seeded and finely chopped jalapeño

Grated zest of 1 lime

1 tablespoon fresh lime juice

1 teaspoon honey

Pinch of crushed red pepper flakes

—Preheat the oven to 400°F, with a rack in the middle position. Line a sheet pan with parchment paper or foil for easier cleanup, if you like.

—Lightly coat the cut sides of the squash with oil, then season with salt and pepper. Put the squash cut-side down on the pan and roast until just tender, about 40 minutes.

—Meanwhile, in a small bowl, stir together the butter, garlic, jalapeños (to taste), lime zest and juice, honey, red pepper flakes, and ½ teaspoon salt. Check the seasonings.

—Transfer the squash to plates, cut-side up, smear each half with some of the jalapeño-lime butter, and serve.

TOMATO AND ZUCCHINI GRATIN

SERVES 6 TO 8

When good tomatoes and zucchini are abundant, you'll want to make this gratin. It takes a little time to cut and arrange the vegetables, but it is worth the effort. The smell of oregano mingling with the roasting vegetables and Parmesan breadcrumb topping can fool us into thinking we're on a sun-drenched terrace in Provence, even when we're folding a pile of laundry at home. On a more practical note, the dish can be served hot, warm, or at room temperature; it reheats well; pairs great with lots of mains, including grilled meats and fish; and can even be a main course itself.

²/₃ cup panko or dried breadcrumbs

¹/₃ cup freshly grated Parmesan or pecorino cheese

2 tablespoons unsalted butter, melted

1 small garlic clove, halved lengthwise

3 medium zucchini (about 1¹/₂ pounds), cut lengthwise into ¹/₄-inch slices

5 medium tomatoes (about 2 pounds), cut crosswise into ¹/₄-inch slices

¹/₄ cup olive oil

2 teaspoons chopped fresh oregano leaves or ¹/₂ teaspoon dried

Salt and pepper

—Preheat the oven to 425°F, with a rack in the lower and upper thirds. In a small bowl, combine the panko and cheese, then stir in the butter and set aside.

—Rub the inside of a 13 x 9-inch baking dish with the garlic. Lay a slice of zucchini crosswise in the dish, followed by a few slices of tomato, overlapping the zucchini. Repeat until you've used all of the vegetables, trimming them and/or creating one or two rows along the bottom of the dish as needed. The arrangement of the vegetables doesn't have to be fussy; just try to spread them out as much as possible. Drizzle evenly with the oil, then top with the oregano. Season generously with salt, then season with pepper. Bake on the lower rack until the vegetables are softened and the juices are bubbling, about 20 minutes.

—Remove from the oven, sprinkle the breadcrumb mixture evenly over the vegetables, then bake on the upper rack until the vegetables are tender and browned at the edges and the top is golden brown, about 15 minutes more. Let cool for 5 to 10 minutes before serving. Serve hot, warm, or at room temperature.

 TIP: You can skip the cheese in the topping, if you like. Just use a total of 1 cup panko or dried breadcrumbs and season with salt.

GREEN BEANS WITH SUN-DRIED TOMATO PESTO BREADCRUMBS

SERVES 4

On particularly hectic nights, we sometimes serve these crunchy, deeply savory beans topped with an over-easy egg and happily call it dinner. Don't worry about precisely measuring out the ingredients for the flavored breadcrumbs—it won't matter if there's a little more or less of something. Use the measurements as a guide and adjust them to suit your taste.

— Bring a large pot of water to a boil over high heat. Meanwhile, in a small bowl, using a rubber spatula or your hands, mash or rub together the breadcrumbs, sun-dried tomatoes, cheese, garlic, and anchovy paste. Season with salt and pepper, then set the flavored breadcrumbs aside.

— When the water boils, season it generously with salt; it should taste like seawater. When it returns to a boil, add the green beans and gently boil, stirring once or twice, until crisp-tender, about 2 minutes. Drain, pat dry, then set aside.

— In a large skillet, heat the oil over medium heat. Add the flavored breadcrumbs and toast, stirring often, until golden brown, about 2 minutes. Add the blanched green beans and cook, stirring often, until coated with the breadcrumbs and heated through, about 2 minutes. Check the seasonings and serve.

$1/2$ **cup dried breadcrumbs or panko**

2 oil-packed sun-dried tomatoes, drained and minced

2 tablespoons freshly grated pecorino or Parmesean cheese

1 small garlic clove, minced

$1/4$ **teaspoon anchovy paste**

Salt and pepper

1 pound green beans

2 tablespoons olive oil

SAUTÉED SUGAR SNAPS WITH RADISHES AND MINT

SERVES 4

This is an almost absurdly simple but reliably rewarding way to dress up sugar snaps. Be generous with the heat and salt from the start and stingy with the cooking time and you'll end up with a bright, full-flavored side dish with a nice crunch. If you don't like mint or don't have any on hand, fresh tarragon and dill are both good substitutes; however, this is an instance where dried herbs wouldn't add anything. You can also skip halving the sugar snaps, if you like.

—In a large skillet, heat the oil and butter over medium-high heat. Add the sugar snaps and radishes, season with salt and pepper, and cook, stirring often, until just crisp-tender, about 4 minutes. Off the heat, stir in the mint, then check the seasonings and serve.

1 tablespoon olive oil

1 tablespoon unsalted butter

$^3/_4$ pound sugar snap peas, halved crosswise on the diagonal

10 radishes, each cut into six wedges

Salt and pepper

Handful of mint leaves, roughly chopped

QUICK-CURED CUCUMBER SALAD

SERVES 4

We make this slightly tart, light, refreshing side dish a lot during the warmer months. Caroline will eat a whole batch by herself standing at the kitchen counter. Kathy always prepares double so there's enough for dinner and lunch the next day (and because she's nicer about sharing with her family).

With their thin skin and small seeds, English cucumbers are ideal here, but you can use regular cucumbers, too. Substitute two and peel them, cut in half lengthwise, and scrape out the seeds before cutting into very thin slices. It takes less than a minute on a mandoline or Benriner slicer (see page 12).

1 English cucumber, very thinly sliced

1¹/₂ teaspoons salt, preferably kosher

2 tablespoons rice vinegar (not seasoned) or distilled white vinegar

1 teaspoon sugar

——In a medium bowl, toss together the cucumbers and salt, using your hands to separate any cucumber slices and to evenly distribute the salt. Let sit until soft and pliable, about 20 minutes. Drain, firmly squeeze out and discard any excess liquid (remove as much liquid as possible or the dish will be watery and too salty), then return to the bowl.

——Add the vinegar and sugar and toss together, breaking up any clumps of cucumber, if needed. Refrigerate, covered, for at least 30 minutes, and up to 3 days. Check the seasonings before serving. The salad should be a little salty-sweet with a slightly tart edge.

GREEN BEANS WITH OIL AND LEMON

SERVES 4

There's no easier, or zingier, way to perk up plain cooked green beans than by tossing them with equal parts olive oil (the good stuff) and fresh lemon juice. This Greek "sauce," called latholemono, is a classic accompaniment to grilled fish and shellfish, but is just as wonderful on grilled or roasted chicken, pork, or lamb, as well as other vegetables such as asparagus, spinach, and broccoli.

You can skip the ice bath and serve the combination hot or warm, if you like. Either way, be sure to dry the beans well before tossing with the sauce or the water will dilute the flavor. And feel free to adjust the amount of oil and lemon juice to suit your taste. Chopped herbs—dill, oregano, flat-leaf parsley, mint—would also be a nice addition.

2 tablespoons olive oil

2 tablespoons fresh lemon juice

Salt and pepper

1 pound green beans

—Bring a large pot of water to a boil over high heat. Meanwhile, in a large bowl, whisk together the oil and lemon juice until combined. Season with salt and pepper and set the sauce aside.

—Fill a large bowl with ice water. Season the boiling water generously with salt; it should taste like seawater. When it returns to a boil, add the green beans and gently boil, stirring once or twice, until crisp-tender, about 2 minutes. Drain, immediately submerge the green beans in the ice water to stop the cooking and retain the color, then drain again when cold and pat dry.

—Add the blanched green beans to the sauce and toss to combine. Check the seasonings and serve. The green beans are best eaten within a few hours.

CUCUMBER AND WATERMELON SALAD

SERVES 4 TO 6

Much as we like the classic watermelon and tomato salad, we like the refreshing combination of watermelon and cucumber even more. They come from the same family of vine-growing plants and complement each other beautifully, especially when mixed with some vinegar and oil, thinly sliced shallots, and shaved pecorino. For an extra layer of flavor and a little crunch, sprinkle the salad with a finishing salt, such as fleur de sel.

1 large shallot, halved lengthwise and thinly sliced

3 tablespoons white wine vinegar

¼ cup olive oil

Salt and pepper

4 cups ½-inch cubed seedless watermelon (from about ½ small watermelon)

2 cucumbers, peeled, seeded, and cut into ½-inch cubes

Wedge of pecorino or Parmesan cheese (about 4 ounces will be used)

—In a large bowl, combine the shallots and vinegar and let sit for 10 minutes to soften the flavor. Whisk in the oil, then season with salt and pepper. Add the watermelon and cucumbers and gently toss to combine. Check the seasonings, then divide the salad among plates. With a vegetable peeler, shave a few long slivers of cheese over each portion, reserving the remaining cheese for another use, and serve. You could also put the salad on a platter and then top with the cheese.

 TIP: If we're grilling when we make this salad, we sometimes throw the watermelon on the grill, too. It gets a smoky edge and tastes more intense. Cut the watermelon into slices so they don't slip through the rack, brush the rack with olive oil, and grill over medium heat until lightly charred, about 2 minutes per side. Cut the watermelon into cubes before mixing with the cucumbers.

CLASSIC CELERIAC SALAD

SERVES 4 TO 6

When we rave about celeriac to friends, they often stare at us blankly before asking, "What's celeriac?" A type of celery grown for its bulbous root rather than its stalks, it's the ugly ducking of root vegetables. Typically found during the cold months in a remote corner of the produce section, this nubby beige-brown orb is often overlooked. But under its rough, mottled skin lies ivory-hued flesh with a mellow, clean flavor that's a cross between celery and parsnip.

Celeriac is a welcome change from potatoes, and just as versatile. Simmer chunks with sautéed chopped onion, celery, and carrots, a bay leaf, and chicken or vegetable broth and puree into a soup; roast them with olive oil, salt, and pepper (see Roast Your Vegetables, page 157); or boil them and mash as you would spuds. You can also shred raw celeriac to make this French bistro staple, called céleri rémoulade. Serve it in place of the fennel salad for Chicken Milanese (page 49), with Pork Tenderloin with Double-Apple Sauce (page 89), or alongside slices of plain baked ham. Or eat it the way Caroline's Belgian mother does: piled between two pieces of crusty baguette.

½ cup mayonnaise

2 tablespoons Dijon mustard

2 teaspoons fresh lemon juice

Salt

Pepper

1½ pounds celeriac, peeled and shredded

Handful of flat-leaf parsley, chopped (optional)

—In a large bowl, combine the mayonnaise, mustard, lemon juice, and 1 teaspoon salt. Season with pepper, then stir to combine. Add the celeriac and parsley (if using) and toss to combine. Check the seasonings and serve.

TIP: When buying celeriac, look for bulbs that are firm and heavy for their size, with no soft spots and few root outgrowths. We prefer celeriac about the size of a softball. Celeriac that are smaller than that are more tender, but they don't yield much after you peel them, and really large ones can be woody. Regardless, celeriac has a tough exterior that must be removed. Use whichever you're more comfortable with: a sharp knife or peeler. To shred, we prefer to use a food processor, but you can also use a box grater. Cutting it in half or in quarters might make it easier to handle.

CLEAN-OUT-THE-VEGETABLE-DRAWER CHOPPED SALAD

SERVES 4 TO 6

Whenever the vegetable drawer is filled with various odds and ends begging for attention, pull them all out, chop them up, and toss them with a mustardy, lemony, garlicky vinaigrette. The sum is greater than the parts, and we find that our kids eat the salad with gusto even when it includes vegetables they normally balk at. With some cured meats, cheese, and crusty bread, dinner is served—and the vegetable bin is emptied.

—In a large bowl, whisk together the lemon juice, mustard, and garlic. Slowly whisk in the oil until emulsified, then season generously with salt and pepper. Add the vegetables and herbs and toss to combine. Check the seasonings and serve.

2 tablespoons fresh lemon juice

1 tablespoon Dijon mustard

1 small garlic clove, smashed

¼ cup olive oil

Salt and pepper

6 cups assorted chopped vegetables (aim for a mixture of at least 3), such as carrots, celery, radishes, daikon, tomatoes, cucumbers, sugar snap peas, zucchini, fennel, or bell peppers

Large handful of flat-leaf parsley or whatever suitable fresh herbs may also be languishing in the fridge, chopped (optional)

RAW CORN SALAD WITH RADISHES, JALAPEÑO, AND LIME

SERVES 4

Raw corn and radishes may seem like an unusual pairing—until you try this addictive salad, which doesn't require any cooking, comes together in minutes, and is as pretty as it is delicious. Use the freshest, sweetest corn possible; a pinch of sugar or drop of honey will help kernels that are lacking in sweetness. (See page 152 for a Tip about cutting kernels from an ear of corn.) The olive oil is optional: Kathy thinks the salad tastes cleaner without it; Caroline likes the way it binds the ingredients together.

—In a medium bowl, combine the corn, radishes, jalapeño, cilantro, lime juice, and oil (if using); season with salt and toss to combine. Check the seasonings and serve. The salad can be refrigerated, covered, for up to a day, but is best eaten soon after tossing because it loses its crunch and the radishes start to bleed.

3 cups fresh corn kernels (about 5 ears)

6 small radishes, very thinly sliced

$^1/_2$ jalapeño, seeded and finely chopped

Handful of cilantro, roughly chopped

3 tablespoons fresh lime juice

$1^1/_2$ tablespoons olive oil (optional)

Salt

TIP: If you'd like to prepare the salad ahead of time, assemble all the ingredients in the bowl except for the lime juice, oil (if using), and salt. Cover the surface with a damp paper towel, then cover the bowl with plastic wrap, and refrigerate for up to a day. Toss with the lime juice, oil, and salt before serving.

ITALIAN TOMATO-BREAD SALAD

SERVES 6

If we had to name the top 10 dishes requested by our families, this salad would be high on the list. It's our version of the classic Tuscan salad known as panzanella, with some celery thrown in for a bit of crunch and lemon zest and mint for a refreshing kick.

It's common to moisten the bread with water before adding it to the salad, but depending on how stale the bread is and how juicy the tomatoes are, sometimes it's not necessary. So we hold off, mixing the bread with the rest of the ingredients first. Whether or not you add water, be generous with the salt—the tomatoes and bread soak it right up.

1½ pounds tomatoes (about 2 large), chopped and juices reserved

3 celery stalks, halved lengthwise and sliced

½ small red onion, finely chopped

1 large garlic clove, minced

Grated zest of 1 lemon

¼ cup olive oil

2 tablespoons red wine vinegar

Salt and pepper

2 heaping cups ¾-inch cubed stale crusty French or Italian bread

Handful of basil leaves, torn

Small handful of mint leaves, torn

—In a large bowl, combine the tomatoes and their juices, celery, onions, garlic, lemon zest, oil, and vinegar. Season with salt and pepper, then toss together. Add the bread, basil, and mint and gently toss together.

—If the bread is moistened through and there's a small amount of liquid pooling at the bottom of the bowl, no water is needed (see note above). If the salad looks dry, sprinkle some water over the top, gently toss, and repeat if needed. Check the seasonings. The salad is best served within a few hours, before the bread gets too soggy.

TIP: If you don't have any stale bread, you can "cheat" and bake the cubes in a 250°F oven, stirring once or twice, until dry but not browned, about 25 minutes.

ASPARAGUS WITH SESAME DRESSING

SERVES 4

This nutty, slightly sweet Japanese dressing completely transforms blanched cold green vegetables. It's traditionally served with spinach, but is also fantastic on asparagus, as well as broccoli and green beans. If you have kids who will more readily eat vegetables if they can dip them in a flavorful sauce, then double or triple the dressing and serve it in a ramekin alongside the asparagus instead.

1½ tablespoons soy sauce

1 tablespoon sesame oil

½ tablespoon water

½ tablespoon sugar

1½ tablespoons toasted white sesame seeds (see Tip)

Salt

1 pound asparagus, cut on the diagonal into 1-inch pieces

— Bring a medium saucepan of water to a boil over high heat. Meanwhile, in a medium bowl, stir together the soy sauce, sesame oil, water, and sugar until the sugar dissolves. Coarsely grind the sesame seeds with a mortar and pestle (you can also use a spice grinder; if you have neither, add them whole), then stir into the soy sauce mixture and set the dressing aside.

— Fill a medium bowl with ice water. Season the boiling water generously with salt; it should taste like seawater. When it returns to a boil, add the asparagus and gently boil, stirring once or twice, until crisp-tender, about 2 minutes. Drain, immediately submerge the asparagus in the ice water to stop the cooking and retain the color, then drain again when cold and pat dry.

— Add the blanched asparagus to the dressing and toss to combine. Check the seasonings and serve. The asparagus salad will keep, covered in the refrigerator, for about 2 days, but is best eaten the day it's made.

 TIP: White sesame seeds are sold both toasted and raw. The former are fine—and convenient—but we generally buy raw seeds and toast them ourselves as needed to bring out their nutty flavor and aroma. (Use either method described in Toasted Seeds, page 9.) We like being able to control the level of toasting (the darker the color, the more intense the taste), and they're particularly good when freshly toasted.

CARROT, CHEDDAR, AND GREEN APPLE SALAD

SERVES 4 TO 6

This colorful salad, tossed with a honey dressing spiked with thyme, is popular with kids and adults alike. A food processor makes quick work of the shredding, but you can also use a box grater. Opt for packaged shredded cheese, if you like, but we don't recommend packaged shredded carrots; they're often flavorless and watery.

—In a medium bowl, whisk together the vinegar, mayonnaise, mustard, water, honey, thyme, and shallots, then season with salt and pepper. Add the carrots, cheese, apples, and parsley (if using) and toss to combine. Check the seasonings and serve at room temperature or chilled.

2 tablespoons apple cider vinegar

1 heaping tablespoon mayonnaise

2 teaspoons Dijon mustard

2 teaspoons water

1 teaspoon honey

Scant $\frac{1}{2}$ teaspoon dried thyme

1 shallot, minced

Salt and pepper

5 large carrots, shredded

4 ounces sharp cheddar cheese, shredded (about 1 cup)

1 Granny Smith apple, unpeeled, cored, and shredded

Large handful of flat-leaf parsley, chopped (optional)

RAW BEET SALAD

SERVES 4

It may be hard to believe that rock-hard beets taste wonderful raw, but the proof is in the salad. Crunchy and sweet, they pair well with creamy, acidic dressings like the goat cheese one here and also make a great addition to coleslaw, sandwiches, and mixed green salads. We suggest using a sharp Y peeler to remove the skin and, if you like, wearing rubber gloves to avoid staining your skin, unless you don't mind looking like you washed your hands in Hawaiian Punch.

—In a large bowl, whisk together the goat cheese, honey, and vinegar. Slowly whisk in the oil until emulsified, then season with salt and pepper. Add the beets and toss to combine. Check the seasonings and serve.

¹/₄ **cup crumbled goat cheese (about 2 ounces), at room temperature**

2 teaspoons honey

3 tablespoons white wine vinegar

¹/₃ **cup olive oil**

Salt and pepper

4 beets (about 1¹/₂ pounds total), peeled and shredded (see Tip)

TIP: To shred the beets, we prefer to use a food processor, but you can also use a box grater. Cutting them in half or in quarters might make them easier to handle.

ASIAN-STYLE SLAW

SERVES 4 TO 6

Credit for this vibrant soy-sesame-and miso–flavored slaw goes to Kathy's friend Michael Dougherty, a kitchen designer with a flair for entertaining and cooking. Serve it with all kinds of food, including burgers, fried chicken, and grilled steak. Michael suggests making the dressing the night before so the flavors have time to blend. He also uses it as a marinade for meat or fish, first thinning it a bit with some soy sauce and/or mirin (Japanese sweet rice wine).

2 tablespoons rice vinegar (not seasoned) or white wine vinegar

2 tablespoons white miso paste

1 teaspoon grated fresh peeled ginger

$^1/_2$ tablespoon mayonnaise

$^1/_2$ tablespoon fresh lemon juice

$^1/_2$ teaspoon honey

3 tablespoons sesame oil

2 tablespoons grapeseed or vegetable oil

Salt and pepper

6 cups thinly sliced (crosswise) green and/or red cabbage (about 1 small head total)

2 large carrots, julienned or thinly sliced

4 large radishes, julienned or thinly sliced

4 scallions (white and pale greens parts only), thinly sliced on the diagonal

2 tablespoons black and/or toasted white sesame seeds (optional; see Tip, page 178)

——In a small bowl, whisk together the vinegar, miso, ginger, mayonnaise, lemon juice, and honey. Slowly whisk in the sesame oil until emulsified, then the grapeseed oil. Season with salt and pepper and set aside. (You can also make the dressing in a blender.) The dressing will keep, covered in the refrigerator, for about 4 days. Whisk before using.

——In a large bowl, combine the cabbage, carrots, radishes, and scallions. Add a little more than half of the dressing and toss to combine. If the slaw is too dry, add a little more. Check the seasonings, then sprinkle with the sesame seeds (if using) and serve.

STARCHES AND GRAINS

SOFT PARMESAN POLENTA

SERVES 4 TO 6

As soon as there's a chill in the air, we start craving this comforting classic. We'll happily eat steaming-hot bowlfuls topped with only a pat of butter, but it's also the perfect accompaniment to everything from a tangle of sautéed greens and poached eggs to juicy roasts and hearty stews—not to mention a welcome change of pace from potatoes, rice, and noodles.

The slow-cooked variety of polenta turns out creamy and full-flavored with nothing more than water and salt, but our weeknights rarely afford us the time needed to prepare it. So, we use a quality instant brand—Bellino and Campanini are two—and doctor it up. It's fast enough to do anytime, and the end result is good enough that we want to. (The polenta is wonderful with the Parmesan, but you can skip it if you like; or try it with 1/2 cup crumbled Gorgonzola or 1/2 cup mascarpone instead.)

2¹/₂ **cups low-sodium chicken broth**

2¹/₂ **cups whole milk**

1 **scant tablespoon chopped fresh rosemary or 1 scant teaspoon crushed dried rosemary**

1 **cup instant polenta**

2 **tablespoons unsalted butter**

1 **cup freshly grated Parmesan or pecorino cheese**

Salt and pepper

— In a medium saucepan, combine the broth, milk, and rosemary and bring to a boil over high heat. (Watch that it doesn't boil over; it can happen in an instant.) Pour the polenta into the liquid in a slow, steady stream, whisking briskly and constantly until the liquid and polenta are a homogenous mass.

— Reduce the heat so the mixture barely bubbles and stir constantly with a wooden spoon, getting into the "corners" of the pot, until the mixture has thickened and lost its raw cornmeal taste, about 5 minutes.

— Off the heat, stir in the butter and cheese, then season with salt and pepper. Polenta firms up quickly, so serve right away or keep covered in a double boiler over low heat for up to 2 hours.

TIP: Another serving suggestion is to pour the just-cooked polenta into a greased or parchment paper–lined baking dish or sheet pan and refrigerate until cold and firm. The chilled polenta will keep, covered in the refrigerator, for several days, so this is a convenient make-ahead option. When ready to serve, cut it into shapes (triangles, rounds, squares, or even farm animals, as shown on the opposite page) and then sauté or grill until heated through. You can also layer the cold polenta with tomato sauce, cheese, and vegetables or meat and bake it like a lasagna.

EVERYDAY BLACK BEANS

MAKES 5 TO 6 CUPS

Whenever we have a big batch of black beans in the fridge, we smugly go through the day feeling like dinner is practically on the table. It's the same with rice, which is why we generally try to have one or the other on hand. Similar to our Lifesavers (page 217), these fridge staples give us options, building blocks to start from, and that important psychological lift: "Ask me what's for dinner; just ask me!"

Some of our favorite one-step ideas for turning black beans into a meal are: Wrap them in a tortilla; serve over rice; puree and thin out to make a soup; or top with fried or scrambled eggs and salsa. Possible garnishes for those options include sour cream, chopped white onions and tomatoes, cilantro, cheddar or Monterey Jack cheese, and lime wedges. You can also use the beans to make the enchiladas on page 104 or stir them into soups, stews, chili, and vegetable dishes. Of course, you can do all this with canned black beans, too. But while we always have some cans in our pantry, we prefer to use cooked dried beans when possible. They taste better, have a better texture, and are more economical. And once you put the ingredients in the pot, there's little to do except wait until they're done.

1 pound dried black beans (about 2¹/₂ cups), rinsed and picked over

¹/₂ white onion, finely chopped

2 garlic cloves, smashed

1 small jalapeño, halved lengthwise and seeded

Several cilantro stems (optional)

6 cups cold water

1 teaspoon salt

—In a medium saucepan, combine the beans, onions, garlic, jalapeños, cilantro stems (if using), and water and bring to a boil over high heat. Reduce the heat and simmer, stirring occasionally, until the beans are al dente, about 1 hour. Add the salt and continue to cook until the beans are just tender, 30 to 45 minutes more (older beans take longer to cook). If at any point during cooking the beans aren't covered by the liquid, add more water. They should be a little soupy at the end.

—Discard the jalapeños and cilantro stems (if using), then check the seasonings. Serve hot or warm. The beans will keep, covered in the refrigerator, for about 1 week. To reheat, thin with water (beans thicken a lot as they cool) and warm them gently on the stove, stirring occasionally, or microwave them partially covered.

TOASTED ORZO RISOTTO-STYLE

SERVES 4 TO 6

Orzo prepared in the general style of risotto tastes better than boiled orzo, and it doesn't take much more effort. It's also more forgiving than risotto rice, which can get gummy if not cooked properly. Toasting the orzo for a few minutes before adding the broth gives the finished dish a slightly nutty and more complex note.

You could also stretch it into a main course by stirring in some cooked vegetables (asparagus, broccoli, fennel, peas) and/or seafood (shrimp, scallops, salmon). Just add a little more broth or water, butter, and cheese to keep the orzo loose and creamy.

—In a medium saucepan, heat the oil and 1 tablespoon of the butter over medium-low heat. Add the onions and cook, stirring occasionally, until soft, about 8 minutes. Add the orzo and cook, stirring often, until lightly toasted, about 3 minutes.

—Add the water, raise the heat, and simmer, stirring often, until the water is absorbed, about 6 minutes. Add the broth as you would if you were making risotto, a little at a time, stirring constantly and allowing it to be absorbed after each addition, until the orzo is just tender, about 6 minutes more. The mixture should be a little soupy; if not, add a little more broth or water.

—Off the heat, stir in the remaining 1 tablespoon butter, then the cheese. Season with salt if needed (the broth and cheese may have provided enough salt), and pepper, then stir in the lemon zest and parsley (if using). Serve right away, topped with extra cheese, if you like.

1 tablespoon olive oil

1 tablespoon unsalted butter, plus 1 tablespoon

1/2 yellow onion, finely chopped

1 1/2 cups orzo

2 cups water

2 cups low-sodium chicken broth at room temperature, plus extra, if needed

1/2 cup freshly grated Parmesan or pecorino cheese, plus extra for serving

Salt and pepper

Grated zest of 1 lemon (optional)

Handful of flat-leaf parsley, chopped (optional)

BOILED BABY POTATOES WITH LEMON, DILL, AND CRACKED PEPPER

SERVES 4

Generous amounts of lemon juice, dill, and black pepper mixed with butter make these potatoes sing. Loosen the grinding mechanism on your pepper mill; coarse flakes are ideal here, giving more "bite," both flavor- and texture-wise. If you don't have a pepper mill, substitute regular pepper. Also, you can use larger potatoes; cut them into about $1\frac{1}{2}$-inch chunks.

$1\frac{1}{2}$ **pounds small red- or white-skinned potatoes**

Salt

3 tablespoons unsalted butter, cut into 3 pieces

Juice from $\frac{1}{2}$ small lemon

Coarsely ground black pepper

Handful of fresh dill, chopped

—In a medium saucepan, combine the potatoes and enough cold water to cover by about 2 inches. Salt the water so that it tastes like seawater. Bring to a boil over high heat, then reduce the heat and simmer until the potatoes are just tender, about 15 minutes.

—Drain the potatoes and return them to the pot. Place the pot over medium heat, shaking occasionally, to dry out the potatoes, about 1 minute. Off the heat, add the butter and lemon juice and season with salt and a generous amount of pepper. Put the lid on the pot and shake vigorously. You want the potatoes to break up a bit so the flavorings get under the skins. If they need a little help, crush slightly with a fork. Check the seasonings, then add the dill, shake again, and serve. (If you aren't serving the potatoes right away, hold off on adding the dill because it quickly starts to discolor.)

TIP: *When it comes to boiling potatoes and vegetables, we usually drain the water from the pot using the lid rather than a colander: Inevitably, there's no room for such a bulky item in the dishwasher, and its many nooks and crannies make it a pain to clean by hand. Just make sure you have a firm grip on the lid before you tip over the pot.*

NO-FUSS ROASTED POTATOES

SERVES 4 TO 6

There are many recipes for roasted potatoes—some involve par-boiling them first, starting them in a skillet over high heat, or mixing them with a bunch of other ingredients—but ours couldn't be simpler and yields crisp, tender, salt- and herb-flecked nuggets that will disappear as fast as you can serve them. We cut them into chunks no bigger than 1 inch or they'll take longer to cook and won't have the same heavenly ratio of crispy outside to tender inside.

2¹/₂ **pounds potatoes, preferably the small red- or white-skinned variety, cut into about 1-inch chunks**

2 **tablespoons olive oil**

1 **teaspoon salt, preferably coarse sea salt**

Leaves from 2 sprigs rosemary or ¹/₂ tablespoon dried rosemary (optional)

—Preheat the oven to 425°F, with a rack in the middle position. Put the potatoes on an 18 x 13-inch sheet pan and sprinkle with the oil, salt, and rosemary (if using). Using your hands, combine well, then spread the potatoes out across the pan.

—Roast for 30 minutes, then to scrape under the potatoes, use a metal spatula angled down toward the bottom of the pan and toss them around, spreading them out again. If the potatoes stick to the pan, resist the urge to force them up—you'll likely end up with a pan full of mangled spuds; instead, simply cook them for another 5 minutes or so, then try again. After tossing the potatoes, cook them until golden brown, crisp, and tender, 10 to 15 minutes more. Check the salt and serve.

TIP: This recipe is very similar to Roast Your Vegetables (page 157), but we cook these potatoes a little longer because we like them extra crispy. As with the vegetables, though, aside from using too little oil and not enough heat, moisture and overcrowding are the two key reasons roasted potatoes stick to the pan and don't get crisp. Make sure you dry the potatoes well after rinsing them and then pat dry after cutting, too. And if you don't have a pan large enough to accommodate them in a single layer (without cramming them in), divide the potatoes between two pans.

WARM LENTILS VINAIGRETTE

SERVES 4

Tender lentils coated in a mustardy warm vinaigrette is a French classic that is often served as a first course, but goes brilliantly with lots of main courses, too. Try it with the Poached Fillets of the Day (page 26), Salmon in Foil with Spinach and Cream (page 40), or any of the Sautéed Chicken options (page 55). The pancetta adds a salty, meaty flavor, but you can leave it out if you'd like to make this a vegetarian dish.

—In a medium pot, combine the lentils, a large pinch of salt, and enough water to cover by 3 inches. Bring to a boil over high heat, then reduce the heat and simmer, stirring occasionally, until tender, about 30 minutes. If at any point during cooking the lentils aren't covered by at least 1 inch of liquid, add more water.

—Meanwhile, in a large skillet, heat the oil over medium heat. (If you're using bacon, use 2 tablespoons oil.) Add the pancetta and cook, stirring occasionally until just crisp, about 5 minutes. Transfer the pancetta to a paper towel–lined plate to drain, reserving the fat in the pan. Heat the fat over medium-low heat. Add the shallots and cook, stirring occasionally, until softened, about 4 minutes. Whisk in the mustard and vinegar, then set aside. Warm the vinaigrette before adding the lentils, if needed.

—Drain the lentils, reserving about ½ cup of the cooking water. Add the lentils to the vinaigrette and stir. The mixture should be fairly loose; add the cooking water as needed. Stir in the cooked pancetta and parsley (if using), season with salt and pepper, and serve.

1 cup green or brown lentils, rinsed and picked over

Salt

3 tablespoons olive oil

2 ounces pancetta or bacon (about 2 slices), finely chopped

1 shallot, minced

1 tablespoon Dijon mustard

3 tablespoons red wine vinegar

Pepper

Handful of flat-leaf parsley, chopped (optional)

COUSCOUS TWO WAYS

Couscous is the failsafe side dish. A form of semolina pasta, it takes only minutes to make, is very versatile (adjust the flavorings and "add-ins" based on what you're pairing it with and what you have on hand), is economical (particularly when purchased in bulk), and can be served hot, warm, or cold. The basic couscous recipe below makes about two servings without any add-ins, but can be scaled up.

BASIC COUSCOUS MAKES ABOUT 1½ CUPS

—Put the couscous in a medium bowl. In a very small saucepan, bring the broth and a pinch of salt to a boil over high heat, then pour it over the couscous. Tightly cover the bowl with plastic wrap and let stand until the couscous is tender and the broth is absorbed, about 5 minutes. Gently scrape and fluff the couscous with a fork and serve as is (stir in a little butter or olive oil, if you like) or continue with one of the following preparations.

³/₄ cup couscous

1 cup low-sodium chicken broth or water

Salt

COUSCOUS WITH DRIED CRANBERRIES, CASHEWS, AND ORANGE SERVES 4

—Prepare the couscous as directed. Meanwhile, in a small bowl, whisk together the orange zest, orange juice, maple syrup, and oil, then season with salt and pepper.

—Pour the dressing over the warm couscous and gently toss to combine. Add the cranberries, cashews, and scallions and gently toss again. Check the seasonings and serve.

Basic Couscous (above)

Grated zest of ½ orange

2 tablespoons fresh orange juice

1 teaspoon maple syrup

1 tablespoon olive oil

Salt and pepper

¹/₃ cup dried cranberries

¹/₃ cup roasted cashews, coarsely chopped

2 scallions (white and pale green parts only), sliced on the diagonal

COUSCOUS WITH CHICKPEAS, TOMATOES, AND FETA SERVES 4

Basic Couscous (page 195)

$^1/_2$ teaspoon Dijon mustard

1 small garlic clove, minced, then mashed to a paste

$1^1/_2$ tablespoons fresh lemon juice

1 tablespoon olive oil

Salt and pepper

1 heaping cup Sun Gold or other cherry tomatoes, halved

1 cup canned chickpeas, drained, rinsed, and patted dry

$^1/_4$ cup crumbled feta (about 1 ounce)

$^1/_4$ small red onion, finely chopped

Handful of flat-leaf parsley, mint, or basil leaves, chopped (optional)

—Prepare the couscous as directed. Meanwhile, in a small bowl, whisk together the mustard, garlic, lemon juice, and oil, then season with salt and pepper.

—Pour the dressing over the warm couscous and gently toss to combine. Add the tomatoes, chickpeas, feta, onions, and herbs (if using), and gently toss again. Check the seasonings and serve.

BULGUR SALAD WITH DRIED APRICOTS AND PISTACHIOS

SERVES 4

Bulgur is an excellent alternative to couscous, particularly if you want more grains in your diet. It shares many of the same characteristics as couscous (it cooks quickly—though not quite as quickly, is versatile, and can be served hot, warm, or cold), with the added virtues of being more nutritious and having a little more taste and texture. Here, we cook bulgur with a bay leaf and peppercorns for an earthy note, then mix it with dried apricots and pistachios. The resulting salad goes well with a variety of meat and fish dishes and is also an ideal addition to a make-shift mezze-like dinner of store-bought hummus, baba ganoush, olives, and warmed pita.

—In a medium pot, combine the bulgur, broth, peppercorns, bay leaf, and a pinch of salt and bring to a boil over high heat. Reduce the heat, stir once, and simmer, covered, for 10 minutes. Quickly lift the lid and add the apricots, then continue to simmer, covered, until the bulgur is tender and the water is absorbed, about 2 minutes more. Let rest, covered, for about 5 minutes, then fluff with a fork and transfer to a medium bowl, discarding the peppercorns and bay leaf.

—Add the pistachios, parsley, oil, and vinegar, season with salt and pepper, then gently toss to combine. Check the seasonings and serve.

1 cup bulgur

2 cups low-sodium chicken broth or water

A few peppercorns

1 bay leaf

Salt

1/2 cup dried apricots, chopped

1/3 cup roasted pistachios, chopped

Handful of flat-leaf parsley, chopped

2 tablespoons olive oil

3 tablespoons red wine vinegar

Pepper

QUINOA SALAD WITH SHAVED RAW VEGETABLES AND CARROT-GINGER DRESSING

SERVES 4 TO 6

1 cup quinoa, rinsed

2 cups low-sodium chicken broth or water

Salt and pepper

1/2 pound asparagus, very thinly sliced lengthwise

2 large radishes, very thinly sliced crosswise

1/4 pound sugar snap peas, very thinly sliced lengthwise

1/4 pound Brussels sprouts, very thinly sliced crosswise

3 tablespoons olive oil

Fresh lemon juice

1/4 cup toasted pumpkin seeds (pepitas)

1/2 cup crumbled goat cheese (about 2 ounces)

Carrot-Ginger Dressing (recipe follows)

To us, the best salads include warm grains, raw vegetables, creamy cheese, crunchy seeds, and a tangy, slightly sweet dressing. This one has all that and is also so substantial and satisfying that it's an ideal one-bowl meal for those (possibly rare) nights when it's just you and the remote. If you've only eaten Brussels sprouts and asparagus cooked, you'll be surprised at how good they are when raw and very thinly sliced. If you have one, use a mandoline or Benriner slicer (see page 12) to cut them, and the radishes, too; a peeler also works well with the asparagus.

— In a medium pot, combine the quinoa, broth, and a pinch of salt and bring to a boil over high heat. Reduce the heat, stir once, and simmer, covered, until the quinoa is tender and the liquid is absorbed, about 15 minutes. Let rest, covered, for about 5 minutes, then fluff with a fork and transfer to a large bowl.

— Add the asparagus, radishes, sugar snaps, Brussels sprouts, oil, and a big splash of lemon juice and gently toss to combine. Add the pumpkin seeds and cheese, season with salt and pepper, then gently toss again. Check the seasonings and serve with the Carrot-Ginger Dressing. (You can toss the salad with the dressing in the bowl, but it muddies the look a bit, so we prefer to serve it on the side and let everyone help themselves.)

CARROT-GINGER DRESSING MAKES ABOUT 1 CUP

1/2 pound carrots (about 4 medium), chopped

One 3-inch piece of fresh ginger, peeled and roughly chopped

3 tablespoons rice vinegar (not seasoned) or white wine vinegar

1 teaspoon white miso paste

1 tablespoon honey

1 tablespoon sesame oil

Juice from 1/2 lime

1/4 cup grapeseed or vegetable oil

This is our version of the beloved Japanese restaurant classic. It's light and refreshing with a tangy sweetness balanced by a pop of ginger. Use it on salads, vegetables, tofu, or whatever else you like.

— In a food processor or blender, combine the carrots, ginger, vinegar, miso, honey, sesame oil, and lime juice. Pulse, scraping down the sides as needed, until the carrots and ginger are finely chopped. With the motor running, slowly add the grapeseed oil and process until the dressing is almost smooth. Quickly dip a piece of lettuce (or vegetable) in the dressing, shake off any excess, and check the seasonings. The Carrot-Ginger Dressing will keep, covered in the refrigerator, for about 1 week.

FOUR SEASONS OF FARRO

Until recently, farro was pretty hard to find, so we were thrilled when we started spotting it in our supermarkets next to yesterday's darling of the grain world, quinoa. If you aren't familiar with it, here are the CliffsNotes: Farro, also known as Emmer wheat, may be the word's oldest cultivated grain, and the ancestor of all modern grains. It has a firm, chewy texture and a soft nutlike flavor with a touch of sweetness, is low in gluten, and high in fiber, magnesium, vitamins, and antioxidants. Generally used in soups, stews, and salads, farro can be matched with practically any seasoning and ingredient. To cook it, just boil it in salted water for about 15 minutes. (Farro that's not labeled "semi-pearled" or "perlato" might take a bit longer.)

Now that we can readily buy it, we use farro regularly. Here are four seasonal salads that showcase this fantastic grain. The basic farro recipe below makes about three servings without any add-ins, but can be scaled up.

BASIC FARRO MAKES ABOUT 2 CUPS

—In a medium pot, combine the farro, water, and a pinch of salt and bring to a boil over high heat. Reduce the heat, stir once, and simmer, covered, until the farro is tender, about 15 minutes. Drain the farro and serve as is (stir in a little butter or olive oil, if you like) or continue with one of the following preparations.

1 cup semi-pearled or *perlato* farro, rinsed

3 cups water

Salt

SPRING FARRO (ASPARAGUS) SERVES 6

Basic Farro (page 201)

1 tablespoon olive oil, plus 2 tablespoons

1 pound medium asparagus, cut into 1-inch pieces

2 garlic cloves, smashed

Salt and pepper

4 small radishes, thinly sliced

Small handful of mint leaves, roughly torn

Grated zest of 1 lemon, and juice

— Prepare the farro as directed, then let cool slightly. Meanwhile, in a large skillet, heat the 1 tablespoon of oil over medium-high heat. Add the asparagus and garlic, season with salt and pepper, and cook, stirring occasionally, until the asparagus is crisp-tender, about 5 minutes. (Discard the garlic if it starts to go past golden brown; otherwise, wait until the asparagus is done.)

— Transfer the asparagus to a large bowl. Add the warm farro, remaining 2 tablespoons oil, radishes, mint, lemon zest, and a big splash of lemon juice, season with salt and pepper, then toss to combine. Check the seasonings, adding a little more oil and/or lemon juice if needed, and serve.

SUMMER FARRO (TOMATO) SERVES 6

Basic Farro (page 201)

1 large tomato, diced

1/4 pound fresh mozzarella, diced

1 small shallot, minced

Small handful of basil leaves, roughly torn

2 tablespoons olive oil

1 tablespoon red wine vinegar

Salt and pepper

— Prepare the farro as directed, then let cool slightly. Meanwhile, in a large bowl, combine the tomatoes, mozzarella, shallots, basil, oil, and vinegar. Season generously with salt and add some pepper. If possible, let sit for about 15 minutes so the flavors can meld.

— Add the warm farro and toss to combine. Check the seasonings, adding a little more oil and/or vinegar if needed, and serve.

FALL FARRO (APPLE) SERVES 6

—Prepare the farro as directed, then let cool slightly. Meanwhile, in a large bowl, whisk together the oil, vinegar, mustard, and honey, and season with salt and pepper.

—Add the warm farro, apples, apricots, and sunflower seeds and toss to combine. Check the seasonings, adding a little more oil and/or vinegar if needed, and serve.

Basic Farro (page 201)

2 tablespoons olive oil

2 tablespoons apple cider vinegar

2 teaspoons whole-grain mustard

1 teaspoon honey

Salt and pepper

1 firm, sweet apple, such as Honeycrisp or Golden Delicious, cored and diced

Large handful of dried apricots, thinly sliced, or golden raisins

$^1/_4$ cup toasted sunflower seeds

WINTER FARRO (TUNA) SERVES 6

—Prepare the farro as directly, then let cool slightly. Meanwhile, in a very small saucepan, stir together the vinegar, sugar, and salt. Add the shallots and bring to a boil over high heat. Stir, then remove from the heat, cover, and let steep for about 10 minutes. Drain the shallots, reserving the vinegar mixture.

—In a large bowl, add the tuna and flake with a fork into bite-size pieces. Add the warm farro, oil, pickled shallots, 1 tablespoon of the reserved vinegar mixture, and parsley, season with salt and pepper, then toss to combine. Check the seasonings, adding a little more oil and/or vinegar mixture if needed, and serve.

Basic Farro (page 201)

$^1/_3$ cup red wine vinegar

1 scant teaspoon sugar

Salt

2 small shallots, cut crosswise into thin rings

One 5-ounce can oil-packed tuna, drained

2 tablespoons olive oil

Handful of flat-leaf parsley, chopped

Pepper

GREEN SALADS

SALAD 101

Nothing could seem simpler than a green salad, but it's surprisingly easy to end up with a lifeless, overdressed, even gritty one. The following guidelines are all that separate the hits from the misses:

- A mix of different or specialty lettuces is nice, but quality and freshness trump all.

- Carefully wash and dry your greens (we usually use a salad spinner); gritty, bruised, or damp leaves will sabotage even the best lettuce and dressing.

- Use chilled greens; they'll hold up to the dressing better and in our opinion, salads taste better that way.

- Good oil and vinegar are appreciated, but the ratio—the standard is 3 parts oil to 1 part vinegar, but we prefer more of a kick, so 2 to 1 is our sweet spot—and amount of salt are more important; we've had dressings made with plain-old vegetable oil and generic vinegar that were delicious because they were well balanced and well seasoned.

- Dressings need to taste a little strong and salty on their own to compensate for the relatively bland lettuce they'll be combined with.

- Before you toss your salad, quickly dip a piece of lettuce in the dressing, shake off any excess, and taste; does the dressing need more salt, or vinegar/acid, or pepper, or oil? Keep adjusting and checking until you're satisfied. (If you're serving the salad at a party or big dinner, do this in advance so there aren't any last-minute surprises.)

- Use less dressing than you think you need; the greens should be just lightly coated after tossing. You can always add more.

- Toss gently until all the lettuce is evenly coated. Your hands are the best tools for this!

- Serve the salad as soon as it's tossed; it gets soggy quickly.

EVERYDAY SALAD

SERVES 4

This basic salad is what we turn to when we need a little something to round out a meal or we want a touch of green without any extra cooking. The dressing recipe is just a reference point. Once you get a feel for it, eyeball the measurements and embellish depending on your mood and what you're serving the salad with. You might add a minced shallot; a plop of Dijon; a smashed garlic clove; a handful of chopped fresh herbs, such as flat-leaf parsley, tarragon, or chives; a dollop of honey; a squeeze of fresh lemon juice; or some combination of the above. Balance the amount of oil, vinegar, and/or salt accordingly.

—In a small bowl, whisk together the oil and vinegar, then season aggressively with salt and add a pinch of pepper. The exact amount will depend on your oil and vinegar—and your personal preference—but we suggest starting with a scant ¼ teaspoon salt and small pinch of pepper. (Or, in a jar with a lid—see page 208— combine the ingredients, cover, then shake vigorously.) Check the seasonings. The dressing should have a good vinegary bite and taste a little salty. As a final test, quickly dip a piece of lettuce in the dressing, shake off any excess, and taste. If it tastes good, your salad will taste good. Adjust the seasonings as needed.

—Put the lettuce in a large bowl and drizzle about two-thirds of the dressing on top. Toss gently until thoroughly combined. If needed, add more dressing and toss again. Serve right away. (If you'd like to get the salad ready, but aren't serving it until later, another way to do it is to make the vinaigrette in the serving bowl, top it with the lettuce, and toss it when you're ready. It can sit like this for up to an hour or so, covered with a damp paper towel; refrigerate it, if you like.)

2 tablespoons oil (we usually use a not-too-strong extra-virgin olive oil)

1 tablespoon vinegar (we usually use red wine vinegar)

Salt and pepper

6 large handfuls of lettuce, torn into bite-size pieces

 TIP: If you eat salads regularly, it definitely pays to prep the greens in bulk and in advance. Despite the convenience of prewashed bagged lettuce, we try to avoid it; it's generally more expensive than heads of lettuce and not as fresh. And the pretorn pieces are more susceptible to bacteria (think ground meat vs. a steak). We do this admittedly annoying task once a week or so and are thankful every time we reach for the salad bowl.

After washing and drying the leaves, loosely pile about 6 handfuls on two connected paper towels. Loosely wrap the paper towels around the lettuce and slide the package into a gallon-size resealable plastic bag. Gently press any excess air out of the bag and seal it. Repeat as needed. Place the bag(s) in the refrigerator; the lettuce should stay fresh for about 1 week. You can also reuse the plastic bag(s); rinse and let air-dry upside down.

DRESSING ENCORE

Once you've mastered Salad 101 and Everyday Salad, why not add a few more dressings to your repertoire? Along with the basic vinaigrette on page 207, the recipes here are staples in our homes and save us whenever we feel like we're slipping into a salad dressing rut. They follow our preferred ratio of 2 parts oil to 1 part vinegar/ acid, with the addition of flavorings (sweeteners, herbs, and/or savory items like mustard or garlic).

Make enough for a few nights, or, if you eat a lot of salad, keep a couple of different dressings on hand (they're also wonderful to drizzle on grains or roasted vegetables). We find the best way to layer and combine the elements of your dressing is to use old jars. Just as we repurpose squirt bottles to store our Magic Miso-Mayo (page 224), we save old jars for our dressings (see Old Jars Are Good Jars, page 216) and often make them in there, too. Just add the ingredients, put on the lid, and shake it like a maraca. Pour out what you need and refrigerate the rest, always shaking again before using.

Most dressings can be prepared in a jar, but it's particularly handy for ratio-based ones because you can skip the measuring spoons and gauge the amount of each ingredient by looking through the glass. If we're making an egg yolk–based dressing or only enough dressing for one meal, though, we usually use a bowl. And feel free to play with different flavorings—that's one of the best parts of making your own dressing.

We make the dressings on this page in an 8-ounce Dijon mustard jar. Each recipe yields about ¾ cup, which is enough for about 24 large handfuls of lettuce (about 16 "side-salad" servings).

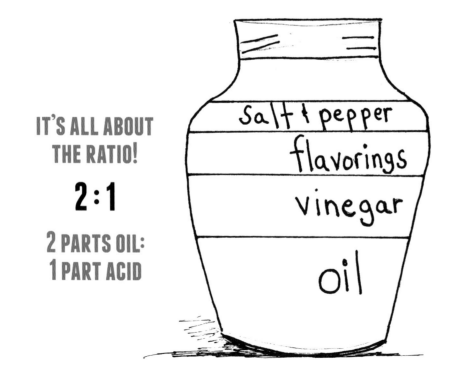

IT'S ALL ABOUT THE RATIO!

2:1

2 PARTS OIL: 1 PART ACID

HOUSE

- ½ cup grapeseed or vegetable oil
- ¼ cup apple cider vinegar
- 1 teaspoon maple syrup
- 1 teaspoon Dijon mustard
- 1 shallot, minced
- Salt and pepper

CREAMY HERB

- ½ cup mild olive oil
- 2 tablespoons red or white wine vinegar
- 2 tablespoons lemon juice
- 2 tablespoons Greek yogurt
- 1 teaspoon honey
- 1 garlic clove, minced
- Large pinch of chopped flat-leaf parsley
- Salt and pepper

ASIAN

- ¼ cup grapeseed or vegetable oil
- ¼ cup sesame oil
- 2 tablespoons rice vinegar (not seasoned)
- 2 tablespoons lime juice
- 1 teaspoon honey
- 1 teaspoon grated peeled fresh ginger (optional)
- Large pinch of chopped cilantro
- Salt and pepper

SALAD 201

The salad-making tips detailed in Salad 101 (page 206) are the foundation for any good salad, but as much as we like a simple bowl of greens, we also like to play with different flavors, textures, and ingredients. Here are some examples:

ADD CARAMELIZED ONIONS. Tossing in sweet, buttery-soft onion slivers is an easy way to elevate any salad. Thinly slice a large yellow onion and cook over medium to medium-low heat in a large skillet with some olive oil, butter, and salt (which adds flavor and helps to break them down and brown more evenly) until supple and deep golden. Stir often and add a little water if the pieces brown too fast; you may also need to lower the heat. When done properly, the process can take up to 20 minutes, so be patient. Let cool to room temperature before using. Any extra will keep, covered in the refrigerator, for about 5 days.

COMBINE RAW INGREDIENTS WITH COOKED. Mixing items such as raw shredded Brussels sprouts, grated beets, or thinly sliced radishes with blanched string beans, steamed peas, or sautéed corn will make a salad more interesting, both taste- and texture-wise.

DON'T ATTACK THE SALAD LIKE A NINJA. We're not fans of salads that resemble vegetal confetti, which seems to be the trend at certain fast-food salad restaurants. What are you eating? Who knows! Aim for bite-size pieces—or a little larger—and lightly toss or layer all the ingredients so every forkful includes something new—and maybe even whole.

MIX IT UP. Try to include flavors and textures that play off each other: salty/sweet, crunchy/tender, chewy/silky—but don't go overboard. There's a difference between exciting and confusing. Some of our favorite add-ins include crumbled feta and goat cheese, dried cranberries and pomegranate seeds, fresh peas and their pods, shredded carrots and blanched asparagus, toasted walnuts and pumpkin seeds, warm quinoa, diced avocado and roasted butternut squash, even whole blackberries (surprisingly lovely in a salad).

RETHINK PASTA SALAD. Sometimes, instead of serving pasta with a salad, we add the tossed greens (arugula is especially good) right on top of the sauced noodles. The combination of flavorful leaves, a bright dressing, and a simple pasta dish (the Angel Hair Pasta with Spicy Tomato-Cream Sauce on page 119, for instance) makes for a delicious union.

ARUGULA WITH RED ONION, PECORINO, AND LEMON

SERVES 4

This is a really flavorful salad we adore, and every time we have it we find ourselves wondering why we don't make it more often—in part because it's so easy that it doesn't even require an actual recipe. The pepperiness of the arugula paired with the salty shaved cheese and smack of lemon even appeals to our kids, although the raw onions they could do without. (And they do, flinging them off their plates like Frisbees.) The olive oil is optional; try it both ways and see which you prefer.

Turn the salad into a meal by topping it with some grilled or roasted shrimp, chicken, and/or vegetables, such as asparagus, zucchini, or red bell peppers.

6 large handfuls of arugula

Thinly sliced red onion

Olive oil (optional)

Fresh lemon juice

Salt and pepper

Wedge of pecorino cheese (about 4 ounces will be used)

—In a large bowl, combine the arugula and onions (as much as you like), drizzle with oil (if using) and a generous amount of lemon juice, then season with salt and pepper. Toss gently to combine, then check the seasonings. The salad should have a lemony, peppery bite; the cheese will lend a little more saltiness. Divide the salad among plates. With a vegetable peeler, shave a few long slivers of cheese over each portion, reserving the remaining cheese for another use, and serve.

TIP: Sometimes we arrange the arugula, onions, and cheese on a platter and set it on the table with a bottle of olive oil and lemon wedges so people can dress the salad as they like.

ICEBERG WEDGES WITH RANCH DRESSING

SERVES 4

If you're one of those people who think ranch dressing is the best condiment since ketchup, this recipe is for you. And despite what roughage snobs may say about iceberg, we have a soft spot for its understated appeal and cool crunchiness; iceberg is also the ideal match for this creamy, tangy dressing.

——In a small bowl, whisk together the buttermilk, yogurt, mayonnaise, oil, vinegar, garlic, and parsley, then season with salt and pepper. (Or, in a 12-ounce or larger jar with a lid, combine the ingredients, cover, then shake vigorously.) Check the seasonings. Quickly dip a piece of lettuce in the dressing, shake off any excess, and check the seasonings again. Put the iceberg wedges on plates, drizzle with the dressing, and serve.

$\frac{1}{2}$ **cup buttermilk**

$\frac{1}{4}$ **cup Greek yogurt**

$\frac{1}{4}$ **cup mayonnaise**

1 tablespoon olive oil

2 teaspoons apple cider vinegar

1 garlic clove, minced, then smeared into a paste

Large handful of flat-leaf parsley or a small handful of tarragon leaves, chopped

Salt and pepper

1 head iceberg lettuce, cored and cut into 4 wedges

RED LEAF LETTUCE WITH MAPLE WALNUTS AND BLUE CHEESE

SERVES 4 TO 6

Composed of a mustard-maple-shallot dressing; buttery red leaf lettuce; sweet, crunchy walnuts; and salty, creamy blue cheese, this salad makes a great lunch or light dinner. You can also round out the meal with some good olives, salumi, and bread. Sometimes we like to stir the blue cheese directly into the dressing, which makes it creamier.

¹/₂ cup walnut halves

1 tablespoon maple syrup, plus 1 teaspoon

¹/₃ cup olive oil

3 tablespoons red wine vinegar

1 tablespoon whole-grain mustard

1 shallot, minced

Salt and pepper

1 head of red leaf lettuce, torn into bite-size pieces

1 cup crumbled blue cheese (about 4 ounces)

—Heat a small skillet over medium-high heat. Add the walnuts and 1 tablespoon maple syrup and cook, stirring often, until the nuts are toasted and the syrup is caramelized, 2 to 3 minutes. Transfer the maple walnuts to a cutting board, let cool for a few minutes, then roughly chop.

—In a small bowl, whisk together the oil, vinegar, mustard, remaining 1 teaspoon maple syrup, and shallots, then season with salt and pepper. (Or, in a jar with a lid, combine the ingredients, cover, then shake vigorously.) Check the seasonings. Quickly dip a piece of lettuce in the dressing, shake off any excess, and check the seasonings again.

—In a large bowl, toss together the lettuce and enough dressing to lightly coat. Divide the salad among plates, top with the cheese and maple walnuts, and serve.

KALE SALAD WITH POMEGRANATE AND PUMPKIN SEEDS

SERVES 4

Okay, raw kale may not sound all that appetizing, but give this salad a try. Massaging (yes, massaging) the leaves transforms them into soft, silky piles and mellows their sharp, bitter edge. Throw in the pomegranate and pumpkin seeds and you have a very approachable, health-ful salad with lots of texture and flavor. If you can find it, use lacinato (also called Tuscan) kale, which is a little sweeter and milder than curly kale, but any variety is fine.

Although seeding pomegranates isn't particularly difficult (see Tip), the convenience of the packaged seeds sold at some stores can't be beat.

—In a large bowl, combine the kale, oil, and salt. Using your hands, massage the leaves, rubbing them with the oil and salt until they become softer, smaller, and darker, about 2 minutes. Taste a piece. If it's bitter, massage a little more. Add the pumpkin and pomegranate seeds and gently toss to combine (don't worry if some of the pomegranate seeds burst). Add the vinegar and toss again. Check the seasonings, adding a little more oil and/or vinegar, if needed, and serve.

1 bunch of kale (about ¾ pound), stems and center ribs removed and leaves cut crosswise into 1-inch ribbons

1 tablespoon olive oil

¼ teaspoon salt

¼ cup toasted pumpkin seeds (pepitas)

Seeds from ½ pomegranate (about ½ cup)

½ tablespoon balsamic vinegar

TIP: Our friend Leslie taught us a no-fuss way to remove the seeds from a pomegranate: Cut the fruit in half crosswise. Hold one half in the palm of your nondominant hand over a medium bowl, cut-side down. Firmly whack the skin with the back of a wooden spoon several times. The seeds should start to fall into the bowl. Continue hitting the skin, gently squeezing the pomegranate a little to help the process if needed, until all the seeds are in the bowl. Repeat with the other half, then discard any white pith that may have fallen into the bowl. In addition to being an effective method, it's good therapy if you're in a bad mood—but we'd still advise not wearing your favorite white shirt.

OLD JARS ARE GOOD JARS

Mustard, jam, gherkin, and honey jars—we love them all. If you were to look in our fridges right now, you'd undoubtedly see a motley (but beautiful) assortment of them, each filled with one of our Lifesavers (opposite page) or some other concoction.

We repurpose glass jars all the time: They're a convenient, BPA-free, and cost-free storage solution for condiments, sauces, dressings, and spreads; their tops seal tightly so we don't have to worry about leaks; they look good enough to function as serving vessels; it's easy to make certain recipes right in them (just pour in the ingredients, screw on the lid, and shake to combine); and, of course, recycling is a good thing. So the next time you've scraped out that last bit of strawberry jam or Dijon, run the jar through the dishwasher, stash it near your oils and vinegars, and use it to make a dressing, etc. Just don't forget to label it (we use painter's masking tape and a Sharpie), and include the date.

LIFESAVERS

These incredibly versatile condiments, which can be made ahead of time (we usually store them in repurposed glass jars; see Old Jars Are Good Jars, opposite page), are refrigerated gold. Just knowing that there's Magic Miso-Mayo at the ready to doctor up a store-bought rotisserie chicken on a frantic Tuesday night (or to make our own roasted chicken taste even better) can instantly drop your stress level a few notches.

AVOCADO SPREAD MAKES ABOUT 1 CUP

This creamy, tangy condiment is terrific on all kinds of burgers, as a replacement for the mayo on a BLT, as a dip for vegetables, even dolloped on scrambled eggs. You can also thin it out with a bit more oil to make a salad dressing. Thanks to the lime juice and vinegar, it won't readily discolor.

——In a food processor, combine the avocado, sour cream, vinegar, lime juice, salt, and a large pinch of pepper. Pulse a few times to break up the avocado, then gradually add the oil with the motor running and process until smooth. (It should have the consistency of mayonnaise.) Transfer to a bowl, then stir in the cilantro and check the seasonings. The Avocado Spread will keep, covered in the refrigerator, for up to 3 days.

1 avocado, pitted and peeled

2 heaping tablespoons sour cream

2 tablespoons white wine vinegar

Juice of $1/2$ lime

$1/2$ teaspoon salt

Pepper

$1/4$ cup vegetable oil

Small handful of cilantro, chopped

- Top any kind of burger or sandwich, BLT, or baked potatoes

- Use as dip for raw or steamed string beans, asparagus, or broccoli

- Layer in quesadillas

- Dress flaked salmon and add to a salad

CARROT-GINGER DRESSING MAKES ABOUT 1 CUP

This is our version of the beloved Japanese restaurant classic. It's light and refreshing with a tangy sweetness balanced by a pop of ginger. Use it on salads, vegetables, tofu, or whatever else you like.

½ pound carrots (about 4 medium), chopped

One 3-inch piece of fresh ginger, peeled and roughly chopped

3 tablespoons rice vinegar (not seasoned) or white wine vinegar

1 teaspoon white miso paste

1 tablespoon honey

1 tablespoon sesame oil

Juice from ½ lime

¼ cup grapeseed or vegetable oil

—In a food processor or blender, combine the carrots, ginger, vinegar, miso, honey, sesame oil, and lime juice. Pulse, scraping down the sides as needed, until the carrots and ginger are finely chopped. With the motor running, slowly add the grapeseed oil and process until the dressing is almost smooth. Quickly dip a piece of lettuce (or vegetable) in the dressing, shake off any excess, and check the seasonings. The Carrot-Ginger Dressing will keep, covered in the refrigerator, for about 1 week.

- Flavor any kind of warm grain

- Dress a green salad

- Use as dip for crudité

- Mix with shredded cabbage for coleslaw

- Top cold or hot tofu

- Toss with cold rice noodles

CHARRED TOMATO SALSA MAKES 1 CUP

Charring the tomatoes and jalapeño give this mild all-purpose salsa a smoky, rich flavor. It may sound strange, but it's also good as a gazpacho-like soup: Scale up the recipe, process the ingredients a little finer, and serve topped with diced avocado and fried tortilla strips, if you like.

—Heat a medium skillet or cast-iron pan over medium-high heat until very hot. Add the tomatoes and chile and cook, turning as needed, until blistered all over and a little blackened in spots. Transfer to a cutting board. Cut the jalapeño in half lengthwise, discard the seeds, and put in a food processor. Cut the tomatoes in half, discard the cores, and put in the food processor. (If you prefer, you can chop the jalapeño and tomatoes—and the garlic and cilantro—by hand instead and combine them with the rest of the ingredients in a bowl.)

—Add the garlic, cilantro, vinegar, honey, and lime juice and season with salt and pepper. Pulse until the ingredients are roughly combined, then add the oil and pulse until just incorporated. Check the seasonings. The Charred Tomato Salsa will keep, covered in the refrigerator, for up to 4 days.

- Serve with any kind of fajita or quesadilla
- Use as you would any tomato salsa
- Stir into scrambled eggs or cooked white beans
- Top crostini or grilled eggplant
- Serve with cooked sausage on a roll
- Toss with pasta

2 tomatoes (about 1 pound)

1 jalapeño or serrano chile

2 garlic cloves, smashed

Handful of cilantro

1 tablespoon apple cider vinegar

1 tablespoon honey

Juice of $^1/_2$ lime

Salt and pepper

$^1/_4$ cup olive oil

CHIMICHURRI SAUCE MAKES ABOUT 1 CUP

This piquant, vibrant green sauce is said to have originated in Argentina, but is popular in many Latin and South American countries. We use it as a marinade for, or accompaniment to, grilled, broiled, or roasted meats, fish, or vegetables. It's also wonderful stirred into white or black beans, on crostini or boiled potatoes, and for sprucing up store-bought rotisserie chicken. There are lots of variations, but we're partial to this one. When we served it at a barbecue recently, one friend said it was so good she wanted to stick her head in the bowl and drink it.

2 garlic cloves, smashed

1 shallot, halved

Large handful of flat-leaf parsley

Large handful of cilantro

Small handful of mint leaves

Pinch of crushed red pepper flakes

3 tablespoons red wine vinegar

1 teaspoon honey

Salt

1/3 cup olive oil, plus extra, if needed

—In a blender or food processor, combine the garlic, shallots, parsley, cilantro, mint, pepper flakes, vinegar, honey, and a pinch of salt. With the motor running, add the oil in a thin, steady stream until it resembles a thin pesto. (If the sauce is too thick and you've added all the oil, add a little more.) Process until combined and a uniform green color, but be careful not to overdo it. You want the sauce to have some texture.

—Check the seasonings. If the sauce needs more acid, add a bit more vinegar and whir again; if it needs more sweetness, add a bit more honey. The Chimichurri Sauce will keep, covered in the refrigerator, for up to 3 days.

• Drizzle on any grilled or roasted meat, fish, or vegetables

• Stir into cooked white beans

• Toss with roasted potatoes

• Top crostini

GINGER-SCALLION SAUCE MAKES ABOUT ¾ CUP

Kathy has been addicted to this piquant, versatile green sauce (think Asian pesto) ever since her first taste at a Singapore hawker stall more than 20 years ago. Who knew the bracing combination of scallions, ginger, salt, and a little oil could be so good? We almost always double the recipe. Once it's in your fridge, you'll keep finding excuses to use it: a dab on steak, fish, or shrimp; mixed into noodles; as a topping on plain rice or with dumplings.

You can whiz the roughly chopped ingredients in the food processor—and sometimes we do—but that tends to break down the scallions, giving the sauce a duller color and a slight slimi-ness. The hand-chopped version requires a little more work, but yields a brighter, more textured sauce. (FYI, Caroline likes to add a splash of soy sauce to the Ginger-Scallion Sauce; Kathy doesn't. Try it both ways and see which you prefer.)

— In a small bowl, stir together the scallions, ginger, salt, and oil. Let sit for about 15 minutes, then check the seasonings. It should almost be "salty." The Ginger-Scallion Sauce will keep, covered in the refrigerator, for about 3 days.

- Serve with steak or seafood
- Use with dumplings
- Top steamed rice
- Mix with soba or udon noodles
- Add to a vegetable stir-fry
- Toss with roasted vegetables like asparagus or green beans or grilled shrimp

1 bunch of scallions, very thinly sliced (about ²/₃ cup)

¹/₄ cup finely minced peeled fresh ginger

¹/₂ teaspoon salt

¹/₃ cup grapeseed, peanut, or vegetable oil

MAGIC MISO-MAYO MAKES ABOUT ½ CUP

The inspiration for this lip-smacking condiment is a miso mayonnaise we discovered at a fancy pants food shop that quickly became habit forming. After tiring of schlepping to the store for our fix (and always leaving with a cartful of items we had no intention of buying), we created our own version, which we like even better. Store it in a squirt bottle (recycle a plastic mayonnaise or ketchup container) and put it on basically EVERYTHING: burgers, sandwiches, eggs, crudités, rice dishes, grilled steak or fish, directly into your mouth. . . . You can double or triple the recipe depending on how much you fall for it.

½ cup mayonnaise

1 teaspoon white miso paste

Fresh lime juice

—In a small bowl, stir together the mayonnaise, miso, and a squeeze of lime juice until smooth. Check the seasonings. The Magic Miso-Mayo will keep, covered in the refrigerator, for up to 2 weeks.

- Top any kind of burger (it's particularly good on salmon or tuna burgers) or sandwich
- Serve with roasted or grilled pork tenderloin
- Stir in some Sriracha for a spicy condiment
- Use as dip for boiled or roasted shrimp
- Spread on grilled tofu or steak
- Add to deviled eggs
- Mix with leftover roast or rotisserie chicken for chicken salad

MUSTARD BUTTER MAKES ABOUT ½ CUP

Juicy steak topped with a silky mustard butter sauce is a French bistro classic we adore. This mustardy compound butter is much simpler to prepare, but still gets raves. The butter can be made well in advance and also pairs well with salmon, chicken, pork, lamb, green beans, or asparagus. (For more compound butters, see page 162.)

4 tablespoons unsalted butter, softened

1 tablespoon Dijon mustard

1 tablespoon whole-grain mustard

Fresh lemon juice

1 shallot, minced

½ tablespoon chopped tarragon leaves (optional)

Salt

—In a small bowl, mash the butter with the two mustards and a splash of lemon juice until combined. Stir in the shallots, tarragon (if using), and a small pinch of salt. Check the seasonings. The Mustard Butter will keep, covered in the refrigerator, for up to 1 week or in the freezer for about 2 months.

- Top grilled or roasted meats, salmon, white-fleshed fish, or vegetables
- Stir into mashed potatoes
- Toss with boiled or steamed green beans, asparagus, pearl onions, potatoes, or egg noodles

SWISS CHARD PESTO MAKES ABOUT 1²/₃ CUPS

As great as traditional basil pesto is, it's not the only kind of pesto. Parsley, spinach, sun-dried tomatoes, and even carrot tops can also be used to make pesto—and, unlike the big, fragrant bunches of basil available in the summer, are abundant year-round. You can also sub out the standard pine nuts and Parmesan cheese, which are wonderful but costly ingredients. We particularly like the combination of Swiss chard, cilantro, sunflower seeds, and pecorino; it complements everything from pasta to roast chicken to a grilled cheese sandwich.

Swiss chard stems and ribs are too fibrous for the pesto, but rather than throw them away, sauté them in some olive oil and eat them or use them in a soup or vegetable stock.

—In a food processor, combine the Swiss chard, garlic, lemon zest, a big splash of lemon juice, 2 large pinches of salt, and some pepper. Pulse a few times to combine, pushing down the chard as needed. Add the sunflower seeds and cilantro and pulse until finely chopped. With the machine running, add the oil in a slow stream and process until incorporated. Add a little more oil, if needed. Transfer the pesto to a medium bowl, stir in the cheese, then check the seasonings.

—If you're not using the pesto right away, cover the top with a thin layer of olive oil. The pesto will keep, covered in the refrigerator, for about 1 week. It can also be frozen for up to 1 month; just omit the cheese and add it before using.

- Toss with any kind of pasta
- Use as you would any basil pesto
- Top grilled chicken, grilled or roasted vegetables, pizza, tomato and mozzarella salad, or crostini
- Mix with chopped hard-boiled eggs for egg salad
- Spread on sandwiches, grilled cheese, or corn on the cob
- Stir into vegetable soups or risotto

3 well-packed cups green Swiss chard leaves (stems and center ribs removed), torn into large pieces

3 garlic cloves

Grated zest of 1 lemon, and juice

Salt and pepper

¹/₃ cup toasted sunflower seeds

Handful of cilantro

²/₃ cup olive oil, plus extra, if needed

1 cup freshly grated pecorino or Parmesan cheese

ACKNOWLEDGMENTS

Keepers blossomed over a phone call, but was really years in the making. And without the following people, there would be no book at all. Our deepest thanks and appreciation to:

William Clark, agent extraordinaire, who wisely, calmly, and patiently helped us navigate every step of the publishing process.

Pam Krauss, for saying "Yes!"

Kathleen Hackett, for taking over *Keepers* with equal parts skill and charm.

Kara Plikaitis, whose incredible design talents are matched by her good humor and thoughtfulness.

Chris Testani and Dub Swinehart, the dream photography duo, for taking beautiful shots despite head colds and a thieving terrier.

Rhoda Boone, for sharing the kitchen with such grace under pressure.

Amy Wilson and Nina Lalli, for their wonderful sense of style.

The rest of our Rodale team, especially Yelena Gitlin, Nancy Bailey, and Kate Slate, for all their hard work, support, and motivation.

Our former *Saveur* colleagues—Colman Andrews, Christopher Hirsheimer, Ann McCarthy, Margo True, Melissa Hamilton, Kelly Alexander, Julie Pryma, Judith Sontag, Shoshana Goldberg, and too many others to list—for being as food-obsessed as we are and for making it so much fun to go to work every day.

The first group of moms we met with, who, over (homemade!) pizza and wine, shared their cooking hopes and woes that helped shape the heart of this book.

Kathy would also like to thank:

The friends I see regularly and those I wish I could, for their encouragement, answering all those questions about dinner in their homes, and knowing when NOT to ask how the book was going.

Jenny Glasgow, who helped me survive my first restaurant job and whose hospitality I'll never be able to repay.

Dorothy Cann Hamilton and the International Culinary Center deans and chef-instructors, for an amazing education that cemented my career path.

Daniel Boulud, the most generous chef I know, who gave me confidence as a young cooking school graduate and who remains a source of inspiration.

Mike Anthony, who has taught me so much about cooking in such a short time and who always reminds me that there's so much more to food than what's just on the plate.

Dorothy Kalins, publishing legend and my mentor. She makes everything seem possible.

The Brennan, Takeuchi, and Steinberger families, especially my mom, for countless lessons in the kitchen and shared meals at the table and for many more to come.

Mike, James, and Ava, who, ironically, never ate worse than when I was working on this book and who far too often had to hear me say, "I'm sorry, I can't. . . ." Your endless understanding and love made *Keepers* possible. You're the bestest.

Caroline, for all those conversations and for bringing *Keepers* to life with me. I couldn't have found a better partner and look forward to continuing our talks long into the future.

Caroline would also like to thank:

My home-cooking sounding board who gamely answered all of my straw polls regarding kale and beyond and provided encouragement, advice, and humor whenever necessary during the long process of writing this book: Leslie Robarge, Sujin Beckerman, Julie Stone, Cathi Allebe, Karin Norby, Nichole Norby, Maya Baran, Felicia DiSabato, Isabel Corbin, Holly Shockley, Jamie Murphy-Meadow, Jill Turpin, Tim Ryan, Laura Simpson, Lezlie Kleitsch, Megan Morse Barbour, Radhika Shroff, Katie Magnuson, Amy Spitzenberger Perry, Kathy Schmidt, Jenny Feldman, Ayana Byrd, Claire Shadood, Lily Henderson, Karen Tyrell, Erica Jung, Mei Chin, Martha Maristany, Suzanne Donaldson, Noah Dreier, Lauren Brody, Wendy Naugle, and Suze Yalof Schwartz.

Bennett Haynes and Ralston Farm, for photo-shoot eggs and the wonderful vegetables that went into the recipe testing for this book.

My grandparents, Grandma and Grandpa Fennessy and Mamy and Papy Allebé, who taught me that perhaps the ultimate happiness is preparing a meal for your family, whether it's waterzooi or an Oscar Meyer weiner.

My Minnesota family, Sue, Joe, and Ruth Campion, who've endured countless epic food excursions and introduced me to the Jucy Lucy.

My children, Belle and Conor, who thought this book would never be done. I love you.

My father, for teaching me how to make the perfect rare steak and to never leave my knives in the sink.

And most important, my mother—without your grace, love, and daily assistance, my life and household would be a wreck. Absolutely nothing is possible without you.

Kathy, my half-Irish sister in all things culinary, for bringing such diligence, flavor, and soul to our book project.

recipes by category

Extra-Fast

All our recipes are weekday friendly, but these take the least amount of effort and time.

Popular with Kids

We can't promise that all of these dishes will be hits with your kids, but we've had success serving them to ours and their friends; we've also included side dishes that complement buttered pasta or a piece of plain chicken or steak.

One-Dish Meals

One-dish meals not only make for an easy dinner with minimal cleanup, they generally reheat well—some, like the chili, even improve once the flavors have had time to meld—so can be prepared ahead of time, too.

Vegetarian

For those who don't eat fish or meat, although dishes marked with a * have fish or meat options; we've also included side dishes and salads that are hearty enough to be served as a main course.

Huevos Rancheros (page 100)

Crustless Broccoli and Cheddar Quiche (page 103)

Black Bean and Butternut Squash Enchiladas (page 104)

Crispy Tomato and Cheese Quesadillas (page 105)

Expat Fried Rice* (page 106)

Pizza Salad* (page 109)

One-Bowl Summer Spaghetti (page 112)

Penne with Broccoli Rabe, Garlic, and Crushed Red Pepper Flakes (page 114)

Spaghetti with 10-Minute Basic Tomato Sauce (page 118)

Angel Hair Pasta with Spicy Tomato-Cream Sauce (page 119)

Fusilli with Zucchini, Gruyère, and Breadcrumbs (page 121)

Rigatoni with Swiss Chard Pesto (page 123)

Farfalle with Gorgonzola, Ham, and Peas* (page 124)

Kale Carbonara (page 126)

As-You-Go Tomato Soup with Quinoa (page 134)

All the Toasts except for Chorizo and Aioli and Curried Chicken and Mango Salad (page 142)

Tomato and Zucchini Gratin (page 164)

Green Beans with Sun-Dried Tomato Pesto Breadcrumbs (page 165)

Italian Tomato-Bread Salad (page 176)

Couscous Two Ways: with Dried Cranberries, Cashews, and Orange and with Chickpeas, Tomatoes, and Feta (page 195)

Bulgur Salad with Dried Apricots and Pistachios (page 197)

Quinoa Salad with Shaved Raw Vegetables and Carrot-Ginger Dressing (page 198)

Red Leaf Lettuce with Maple Walnuts and Blue Cheese (page 212)

Staggered Dinner Times

Ideal for those nights when people will be eating at different times, these dishes (except for the salmon) can be left on the back of the stove and reheated as needed; those marked with a * are also good at room temperature, but generally speaking, cooked foods should be placed in shallow containers and refrigerated within about 2 hours.

Salmon in Foil with Spinach and Cream (you can prewrap, refrigerate, and bake as needed) (page 40)

Morning Chicken* (page 44)

Chicken and Root Vegetable Dinner in a Pot (page 46)

Coconut Chicken Curry (page 47)

Maple Barbecue Drumsticks* (page 50)

Adobo-Style Chicken Wings (page 53)

Chicken and Rice with Ginger-Scallion Sauce* (page 58)

Roasted Chicken Breasts with Sweet Potatoes* (page 60)

Smoky Turkey Chili (page 64)

London Broil* with Chimichurri Sauce (page 75)

INDEX

Underscored page references indicate sidebars and recipe tips. **Boldface** references indicate photographs and illustrations.

THE KEEPERS MANIFESTO

Our philosophy on food, shopping, cooking, family meals, and, what the heck, life in general. Here goes:

1. A sharp knife is safer than a dull one—and much more pleasurable to use.
2. Do you have a fire extinguisher? Is it in the kitchen? Do you know how to use it? Just in case the broiler ignites the chicken, make sure you're prepared.
3. Fancy kitchens don't mean better cooking or better food. Some of the best home cooks we know can whip up a feast with little more than a hot plate. That said . . .
4. A working kitchen should still be a beautiful kitchen: A pretty plant on the windowsill, a favorite ceramic bowl on the counter, Mumford & Sons/Schubert/the Clash (whatever you're into) streaming through the speakers can turn even the most humble space into one that you want to spend more time in.
5. A splash of lemon juice, or any acidic ingredient, can brighten almost any dish.
6. Use more fresh herbs (growing your own is economical and convenient, particularly if they're on a kitchen windowsill). A sprinkle of chopped parsley, chives, or thyme can elevate even the simplest preparations.
7. Organic, free-range, local, etc., are great options but can wreak havoc on your budget. Buy them when it really counts. Hormone-free milk and eggs? Yes. Organic ketchup and Oreos? Not so much.
8. The freezer aisle is good for a few things—peas, ice cream, mini-waffles, and puff pastry. Oh, and ice.
9. Who doesn't like an *amuse-bouche*? Crackers with a hunk of cheddar, apple slices with almond butter, or hummus with carrots can make everyone a little less restless while they wait for you to finish cooking.
10. Hot pan, two slices of buttered bread, your favorite cheese, and maybe some juicy tomato or peppery arugula in between = instant dinner bliss.
11. Let the kids set the table as soon as they're steady on their feet.
12. Wear shoes when you cook.
13. Perfection is way overrated, especially at 6 p.m. when everyone is tired and hungry and you are the only one trying to figure out what to cook for dinner.